Step by Step: A Guide to Stepfamily Living

by

Don Martin, Ph.D.

and

Maggie Martin, Ed.D.

Step by Step: A Guide to Stepfamily Living

Copyright 1992
Educational Media Corporation®

Library of Congress Catalog Card No. 92-070822

ISBN 0-932796-38-9

Printing (Last Digit)

10 9 8 7 6 5 4 3 2 1

No part of this book may be reproduced or used in any form without the expressed permission of the publisher in writing. Manufactured in the United States of America.

Publisher—
Educational Media Corporation®
P.O. Box 21311
Minneapolis, MN 55421—0311

Production editor—
Don L. Sorenson, Ph.D.

Graphic Design—
Earl Sorenson

Dedication

To Paige, Sean and Erin

About the Authors

Don Martin, Ph.D.

Dr. Don Martin is coordinator of the graduate program in counselor education at The Citadel in Charleston, South Carolina. A psychotherapist for over fifteen years, Don has a private practice in marital and family counseling and has been a consultant to numerous mental health agencies and school systems. In addition to professional articles and books, Don has published in popular magazines including *Shape*, *Modern Bride*, *Focus on the Family*, and *Today's Health*, as well as appearing in *USA Today*.

Maggie Martin, Ed.D.

Dr. Maggie Martin is a professor of counselor education at South Carolina in Orangeburg, South Carolina. A former school and mental health counselor, Maggie has a private practice in child and family counseling. In addition to numerous publications in professional journals, Maggie regularly publishes in popular magazines with her husband, Don.

Throughout the year, Don and Maggie are actively involved in parenting presentations and also workshops for professional groups. Anyone interested in contacting them may do so by writing to them at PO Box 34, Citadel Station, Charleston, SC 29409 or call (803) 556-5977.

Table of Contents

Chapter 1
 Understanding the Stepfamily 1
Chapter 2
 Coping with Divorce 9
Chapter 3
 Beginning New Relationships 21
Chapter 4
 Preparing for Remarriage 31
Chapter 5
 The Role of Children When a Couple
 Decides to Remarry 43
Chapter 6
 The Influence of the Ex-Spouse on Remarriage 53
Chapter 7
 Integrating the Family 63
Chapter 8
 Establishing a Stepfamily Lifestyle 73
Chapter 9
 Old Memories and the Stepfamily 83
Chapter 10
 The Role of the Custodial Parent 95

Chapter 11
    Dilemmas of the Stepparent 111
Chapter 12
    Preventing Friction in the Stepfamily 121
Chapter 13
    Creating a Family Atmosphere 133
Chapter 14
    Understanding Children's Behavior
    in the Stepfamily 145
Chapter 15
    The Effects of Relatives, Professionals,
    and Society on the Stepfamily 163
Chapter 16
    Creating Your Own Future 175
References 186

Chapter 1
Understanding the Stepfamily

Families are changing. Across the nation children, close friends, and relatives all show the effects of the changing family in our culture. The traditional family—with a father and mother who are the biological parents of the children—is being superseded by a new type of family called the stepfamily. In a stepfamily, one of the parents is a stepparent and the children may live full-time in the family or visit frequently or infrequently.

Stepfamilies are increasing in number and importance in this country. In approximately 15 percent of American families, one parent is not biologically related to the children. More than 15 million children and about 25 million adult parents live in stepfamilies. Nearly 40 percent of all children will encounter divorce, one in four will live with a stepparent before they reach age 16, and probably a third of all children growing up today will be part of a stepfamily before they reach age 18. Combined with recent estimates that nearly one out of every two first marriages and a higher percentage (56%) of second marriages end in divorce, the tremendous impact the stepfamily is having on our culture becomes clear. Indeed, at its present rate of increase, the single parent family and the stepfamily may soon replace the traditional family as the dominant form of family in America.

Yet the stepfamily is rarely accepted by American society. There are no cultural norms, no rules, and no models for the stepfamily, and its existence has been virtually ignored.

Having worked with stepfamilies for many years, we have found that individuals of stepfamilies are concerned about how to help their families and how to reduce some of the difficulties they face. However, the stepfamily faces hurdles that are different than those of traditional families.

Chapter 1   Understanding the Stepfamily

The Loss of Intimate Relationships

Stepfamily members have suffered the loss of an intimate relationship. Whether through divorce or death, children and adults need to mourn and move beyond this loss. While this makes sense, it is not easy to do. Coping with the pain of saying goodbye or changing the structure of an intimate relationship causes severe strains on most people. Stepfamily members often blame themselves, and sometimes their parents, for their problems.

It is not unusual for a parent to experience emotional, psychological, or physical difficulty in separating from an ex-spouse. The problem is worsened by the ex-spouse who may or may not be remarried, but who still desires attention or who wishes to keep the old ties intact. This usually causes jealousy in the new spouse, and conflict and arguments for everyone else. One spouse typically feels "stuck in the middle" as he or she tries to mediate and please everyone. Pleasing the ex-spouse may be caused by feelings of guilt and the realization that life will never be the same for the person who is alone. When the adults believe that they have disrupted the lives of the children, their guilt is deepened.

Children also have difficult adjustments to make in stepfamilies. They may experience feelings of hurt and loss, and, unlike adults, may have trouble expressing their feelings. Instead of feeling sad, children may get very angry and displace their frustrations on a stepparent. Sometimes simple situations will cause painful memories to be awakened. This only leads to more anger and bitterness, which is often directed at the stepparent.

Mixing Old and New Family Traditions

While old traditions are preserved, new traditions must be created for the stepfamily. Stepfamily members bring memories of their previous families to the stepfamily. Since they have been a part of a family before, they have their own expectations of what the new family should be like.

While maintaining part of the past is necessary for continuity, especially for children, focusing too much on old traditions can cause problems for the members of stepfamilies. Developing customs and common experiences helps families grow closer and to form strong bonds. Talking about common memories creates ties between members even if the experiences were difficult to manage.

Following are some of the more common problems that arise from the past.

Problems in disciplining children.

Parents may not agree about discipline. The children may not listen to the new parent, or the new parent may not wish to become involved in a parental role. The ex-spouse may have trouble accepting the involvement of the new parent or may wish to play a major role in the child's everyday affairs.

The learning of new ways of behavior.

Old rituals regarding eating, dressing, room cleaning, and various other routine chores may be questioned. The new parent and the biological parent may wish to change things because of past problems, or simply because the old ways remind them of the ex-spouse. However, the children may resist this, preferring to "keep things as they were." Sometimes the biological parent may have felt inadequate as a parent and wants the new parent to take the lead with the children. The children sense this and usually resent the new disciplinarian. They may complain or even try to bring in the ex-spouse as a savior.

Changes that nobody anticipates.

If there is one thing that you can expect to happen in a stepfamily, it is that nothing will go smoothly for very long. There are simply too many adjustments to make.

One new stepparent we counseled had the same dream over and over again. In the dream he would be smiling and having a good time. Suddenly, everyone would disappear, or he would think of sad experiences. He felt that his family was the same as his dream. Sometimes he feared that they would all leave him and that he would be all alone with no one to love. At other times, he thought that he could.

Stepfamilies often experience what we call the "roller coaster" effect. They have erratic beginnings and many ups and downs as they try to achieve stability and harmony. Typical examples of the unexpected include:

- An ex-spouse who wants to renegotiate custody.
- Children who leave to live with the ex-spouse.
- A non-custodial father who moves 2,000 miles to another city.
- Child-custody support that abruptly ends.
- A teenager who runs away from home because of a disagreement with the new parent.

While these are just a small sampling of problems that can occur, they illustrate well how stepfamilies must often deal with more stress than traditional families. On top of this, emotional or psychological help is usually minimal or absent from relatives or the community. Although many traditional families feel alone in their struggles to cope with life's problems, this isolation is more intense in the stepfamily.

The differing needs and expectations of family members.

When the members of a stepfamily come together, they often come with different needs and expectations. For example, children may not want a new parent. Sometimes the new parent does not want to be involved with the children. The spouses of a stepfamily may have confusing expectations for each other, because they are not sure how to act. After all, for one of them at least, the previous marriage ended in failure. A prevalent attitude in many second marriages is, "I'll never let you take advantage of me like my first spouse did!" Sensing this in each other, the new spouses may tread easily, hopeful of not making mistakes. This can easily slip into tentativeness, however, which results in its own problems.

The problem of money.

Just like everyone else, stepfamilies fight over and worry about finances. Typical money problems of stepfamilies focus on:

- A new parent refusing to support the children.
- Resentment over custody money.
- Dual careers and how the incomes are shared.
- Separate money for two families even though there is just one family.
- Resentment because an ex-spouse may become a "sugar-parent" and give the children every material object they want.
- Comparisons between how great it was "back then" and how poor we are now.

A lack of enough money is a tough problem to solve and it can create difficulties in stepfamily relationships. Generally, if a stepfamily is of a higher economic status, its money problems are decreased. We don't believe money is less important to traditional families, but rather that money issues become more difficult to solve in stepfamilies because of the different types of people involved in the family. This is particularly true when one considers the power of outside influences with which stepfamilies must cope. Sadly, most stepfamilies do not have the relationship skills necessary to overcome a lack of financial resources.

Chapter 1　　　　　　　　　　　Understanding the Stepfamily

The Hard Process of Developing Intimacy for Stepfamilies

Many stepfamilies find it difficult to develop a feeling of "familiness," or belonging. They find it hard to develop intimacy. The parts may remain parts and never form a new whole. They are many reasons for this, the most typical being:

- A biological parent maintains power and influence over family members even if this person is not supposed to be involved.
- Difficulties in parents sharing children and with children sharing parents.
- Feelings of pain and loss surrounding the visitation of a parent.
- Conflicts in loyalty for children between biological parents or the new parent and the biological parent.
- Competition between "families" and especially between same-sexed parents.
- A parent who is suddenly transformed into a magical hero by the children.
- New relatives appearing overnight as children try to figure out who sees them next.
- The lack of a legal relationship between the stepparent and the new child.

All of these factors make integration a process of time, hard work, and endurance. Unfortunately, many stepfamilies do not have the time to wait for things to get better. Frustrations may be high, and conflict that is inherent in the stepfamily is difficult for people to understand.

Over the years we have found that members of stepfamilies cope with a myriad of problems as they try to create a healthy atmosphere for both adults and children. Understanding the forces and pressures involved empowers stepfamily members to take the steps needed to attain stability, growth, and harmony in their family.

Chapter 2
Coping with Divorce

Many stepfamilies begin with divorced partners. This is one of the most significant ways that stepfamilies are different from traditional families. The individuals in stepfamilies have often experienced divorce and remarriage.

The word "divorce" carries with it many meanings. For some people it means failure; for others it means relief. Most, however, consider it to be a mixed blessing. During the last few decades divorce has become quite common, and even accepted in America. Millions of adults suffer through divorce each year. In fact, present statistics show that nearly 50 percent of the marriages in this country end in divorce. Many of these marriages have children and most of the adults choose eventually to remarry and thus create a stepfamily.

For most people divorce is one of the most difficult and emotional experiences they will encounter. Certainly it is one that most people do not want to repeat. Sadly enough, many do. As therapists, we believe that second divorces can be avoided. However, it takes some introspection and commitment to make the second marriage successful.

> *Joan had been divorced three times and was heading for her fourth. A dominant and persistent woman, her career was always the most important part of her life. Relationships were secondary. As she reached the top of her profession, she realized that there must be more to life than power and money. She had grown distant from both her children and her present husband. She felt lonely and sensed that something was missing in her life. Joan had not learned what it was like to develop a close relationship with someone; she had never learned to give of herself. At last, she was tired of her past patterns and wanted to change.*

While working with couples, we see individuals hamper their present relationships by not confronting and dealing with their pasts. Certainly not all divorced individuals need to relive their past traumas *a la* Freudian analysis, but, for many, the mistaken notions that they have from previous relationships carry right into the present ones. They wind up repeating their previous mistakes.

> *Joe is a good example. He left his first wife because she became too involved in her career and "neglected" their home. During the years that followed, Joe believed that he had come to terms with this problem and he again married a successful woman who enjoyed her work. After a year of marriage, he was considering divorce again.*
>
> *Although Joe had thought he understood what had gone wrong the first time, in reality he failed to grasp that he was looking for an impossibility. On the one hand he desired a self-sufficient woman who could make decisions and earn a good salary. On the other he wanted someone who would take care of him and manage all the household chores. He sought a miracle worker. He was looking for the beautiful woman in the TV commercial who not only brings home the bacon, but cooks it and cleans up her husband's mess, while smiling the entire time.*

In our work, we get angry at the way many people act during divorce, especially when children are involved. It seems like everyone has a stake in the divorce (friends, relatives, lawyers, the I.R.S.), and everyone gives advice to the husband and wife as to how to get as much as possible from the spouse. But that kind of advice only makes the divorce bitter and messy. Ending a relationship and admitting that one has failed (and everyone hates to fail) is trauma enough for most of us. Having children involved in the process only complicates matters.

Often we have seen couples remain in a relationship because of the children. That is usually a mistake. Miserable people make miserable parents and sometimes they help create miserable children. Let us take a look at the cycle.

Parents are strong role models. Statements like "He walks just like his father," or "She talks just like her mom," are common. Living with someone for many years helps shape patterns of behavior, particularly if you are teaching a child the way to adulthood. And that is what parents are supposed to do. The people that children come to know best and believe in are usually their parents.

In our work with families, we believe the strongest force in any family is the couple and their marriage. There is an old saying among family therapists: "If a child is disturbed, the marriage is almost always in trouble." However, if a marriage is disturbed, the kids do not always come out disturbed. Simply put, this means that when we see parents who come to us and say Johnny or Susie is a problem, we know that the marriage is shaky and needs help. So far, we have rarely been proven wrong.

Sometimes a couple comes in and we soon realize that the marriage has severe problems, but the kids seem fine. Some children have an enormous capacity for coping. Still, it takes much work and energy for a child to ignore his or her parents. It is hard enough being a kid without having to figure out that your parents are leading you on the path to unhappiness. It is sad that parents pass down to their children such attributes as child abuse, incest, alcoholism, wife beating, and numerous other afflictions that travel in families for generations. Although divorce should never be viewed as a cure-all, for some families the escape it provides is the best measure.

Even so, divorce is worthless if one does not learn anything about oneself during the process. Sally, for instance, at the age of 11 suffered in an incestuous relationship with her father. At 16 she married a man who abused and beat her. The marriage lasted five years. After running away in fear, she was granted a divorce and ended up marrying two more abusers within a span of three years.

When Sally became involved in a single parent group, she realized that her problems were not just related to being a single parent. She had to learn to get through her past and respect herself as a human being. She had to see that she was worth something and that she did not deserve to be misused. That lesson took Sally years to learn, just like it had taken her years to believe that she was worthless. After more years of pain and torture, Sally finally understood that she could be happy if she worked at it. It was not easy, but she finally became the victor and not the victim.

Most of the people who divorce are not alcoholics, child abusers, or uncaring or insensitive. For a variety of reasons, most simply are not happy with their spouses. When unhappy couples have children, the adults inevitably face the question: "Why not stay together for the children?"

There are plenty of reasons. If a couple stay married for the sake of their children, they usually send their children several negative messages, including:

- Relationships and marriages are unhappy affairs that generally make people sad.
- Most couples fight all the time and bicker over silly, inane matters.
- That women or men are insensitive, irritable, nasty, jealous, spiteful, cold, selfish—the list goes on and on.
- Children are the major focus in marriage; the couple's relationship is of secondary importance.

Brad and Julie had been married for ten years and had two children. Their daughter was eight and their son was five. Their friends thought that they shared a happy marriage. Like many couples, though, Brad and Julie hid their problems from everyone, including themselves.

As individuals they seemed agreeable and friendly. Brad was a salesman and traveled quite often. Julie was a schoolteacher, who attended graduate classes. Because Brad often worked late, Julie assumed most of the duties in the home and with the children. This was fine in the beginning, but eventually it took its toll on the relationship. Julie grew resentful and forced Brad to become more involved with the children. They argued bitterly over this, unwilling to admit that their marriage was deteriorating.

As the children grew up, Julie became more involved in outside activities and tried to gain from her friends what she was missing in the marriage. She seemed to have less and less in common with Brad, and their life together grew boring despite the horrendous fights. Although both agreed to stay together for the children, it did not work. Toward the end of their relationship, they fought constantly and also verbally abused their children. When Julie found someone else, the marriage ended.

Even though divorce usually hurts spouses and children, in most cases it is the best decision for those involved. Most couples work hard to make their marriages successful. It is only after years of struggle that people begin to believe that divorce is the only option left. Seldom is it a quick, easy way out taken by the selfish. Indeed, rarely have we found divorce to be a simple decision. We have found that it takes years for the average person to think about ending a marriage. Many couples in fact separate three, four, or five times before they make the decision to divorce.

Arnold Lazurus, from Rutgers University, recently shared in a workshop about a couple he counseled who were in constant conflict and desired help. Through hard work and effort, the couple learned how to amicably discuss all of the things that they could not agree on. Finally, they stopped fighting and learned how to talk to each other. After all this work, they walked into the counseling office and the husband said, "Dr. Lazurus, you have helped us and have done a terrific job. But we wonder if it is worth it. We still have great differences. She likes steak and I like fish. I get up early and she gets up late. In other words, we are two very different people. We have learned how to compromise but it takes so much work. I think we have realized that maybe it is time for a divorce."

This couple learned that there is much to say for marrying someone with similar interests, who believes in the things you do. Many couples find this out too late.

Understanding why they got a divorce and the reasons their marriages did not work can be helpful for the people who are considering remarriage, as well as for those individuals who are remarried and are experiencing difficulty. Failure to see why the previous marriage ended makes it likely that the mistakes of the past will be repeated.

Divorce for the Woman

Like many major crises, divorce can leave life in an uproar. For a woman, divorce can be a brutal reminder of the hardness of life. This is especially true when the woman has children. Over 25 percent of American households are headed by women who are single parents with one or more children at home. The average income for unmarried women with children is often below the poverty level. In many cases the poverty is a result of abandonment. The majority of men in the U.S. pay sporadic if any child support.

We have all heard stories of women, with no marketable skills, who are left alone with children to support. While in most cases the woman receives custody of the children with support from the non-custodial parent, in an ironic twist, some women have lost custody of the children because they could not support them. Even when they do receive support, many women find that it is not enough.

In addition to the financial struggles and the need to develop a career, women who are single parents face several other difficulties. Now the woman has to do all the things she did before, plus the work her ex-spouse was doing. Along with her previous work and responsibilities, she must learn how to do the jobs that mostly fall to the males: mowing lawns, maintaining the house, car, and appliances, and handling all of the discipline with the children. For some, this experience can be frustrating and defeating; fortunately, for others it can lead to personal growth, a sense of well-being, and security.

Chapter 2 — Coping with Divorce

Janie was married for fifteen years to Frank, a successful doctor. She paid his way through medical school by working as a nurse. Later she worked in his office as a receptionist and nurse. They had three beautiful children, were active in their community, and in many ways seemed to have an ideal marriage. One day, Frank announced that he had found a younger woman, another doctor who was "working her way up the ladder."

The settlement Janie received from her divorce was not enough to pay the taxes on her home. She was bitter and angry at what was left for her after all those years of hard work. But she did not give in to despair. She organized a nursing service with some friends who were in the same circumstances. After several hard, trying years, she started to earn a decent living. However, Janie was luckier than many women her age. She had marketable skills.

Divorce in America is often a bitter contest of wills. In our work with divorced clients, most of them relate the awful mental and emotional experiences of their divorces. We have found that few people part as friends. The more money and children a couple has, the worse the process will be. It is unfortunate that someone with whom intimacy was shared can become such a hated foe.

We see two main reasons for this. One, people have not learned how to withdraw, psychologically and emotionally, from others without hurting them. The rule is to protect ourselves by our anger. People believe you cannot leave someone whom you still love. The philosophy that you can love your spouse and still not be happily married is not accepted by our culture. However, marriage today takes more than love to make it work.

Secondly, if people have not already become adversaries prior to the divorce process, most lawyers will assure that they do during it. Lawyers are trained to defend and win. Their goal is not for husbands and wives to like each other, but to help their clients get the most they can. The destruction of the relationship is not important—money is. Arguments begin over almost anything and everything. Couples fight over houses, cars, pictures, records, silverware, wedding gifts—the most insignificant items suddenly gain major importance. In the end, the client often ends up hating the ex-spouse. For most people, that is divorce in America.

Thus, it is not unusual for divorced women to be suspicious of men in general. For some, anything with a penis is a manipulator, controller, and worthy of being loathed. This attitude is a negative one and generally leads to unhappiness and a waste of energy and resources. It can also lead to great loneliness, but for some women this is easier than facing life's realities. The woman who invests all of her energy into hating men does not have to confront her real problem—how to have a fulfilling, intimate relationship.

It is not much easier for the woman who gains a divorce and remains on friendly terms with her ex-spouse. The difficulties are still many and complicated. This woman finds herself in several dilemmas. She is single, but somewhat married. She is a single parent, yet not entirely single in her parenting.

Indeed, the concept of a single parent is somewhat misleading. The non-custodial parent may have much to say about parenting, wants to be involved in decisions, and even if he or she is 5,000 miles away, that person's presence permeates the family. In many cases, the woman ends up still taking care of the man. She may become burdened with questions like: Is he okay? Maybe I should help him work out a better relationship with the children? Should I drive the children to see him? Women are often very good at taking care of others, and they fall into this role with former husbands rather easily.

Sally is a good example of this. Divorced for three years, her former husband still had a key for the house so that he could see the children whenever he wished. Since he was busy on weekends, she often drove the children 200 miles to see him to keep the father-child relationship strong. In therapy, Sally explored some important questions that she would not face. Was it she, or the children, who needed this relationship? Couldn't he drive a car as well as she? Was she staying attached to her ex-spouse to avoid facing other men? Was she afraid of what her children would say if she started dating? These were difficult questions.

Sometimes women have all the troubles and do not enjoy any rewards. Consider dating. The single woman who has children is treated with caution. The woman mentions that she has children and dates drift away into the moonlight. Should she dare mention marriage with children and dates run into the moonlight.

The road for the divorced woman with children is not an easy one. Some of these women begin to feel sorry for themselves and soon are willing to marry any male who will talk to them. For others, though they can tire of running a house, managing the children and working, they come to like their independence. A man can be a threat to that independence. These women may want roles to change when they date or if they eventually decide to marry again. They want a man not only to accept their children, but to accept them as well. Those terms are far different than the ones that came with the first marriage. Because they do not want to fail at marriage again, these women want things done their way. They want more equality, and more input to the relationship.

In many ways divorced women become new people. And that can become their greatest dilemma—how to develop new relationships when they, themselves, are still developing.

Divorce for the Man

As a man approaches divorce, he, too, feels that he has failed. Love, hate, and anger often are intertwined making it difficult to sort emotions. Most men feel deep disappointment and wonder why they ever got involved with their wives. Although they may inwardly realize that they had a part in the trouble of the marriage, they may want to blame everything on their wives. Most men are beset with uncomfortable thoughts. There is the realization that they will have to start all over again. Maybe they will lose their children? At the least, they realize that their relationships with their children will never be the same.

> *After 20 years of marriage, Gary struggled with all of those concerns. His relationship with his wife Joanne seemed unfulfilling, like much of his life. He had reached a good position in management, but felt that there must be more to life. He tried to explain his feelings to Joanne but she could not understand. With two older sons and a daughter in high school, he decided to leave.*

> He figured that he had several options. He might simply quit his job and start his own business. Or he might travel instead. However, when he told Joanne that their marriage was over she told him that she would get from him all that she could. "I'll be left alone without a job," she said. "I've lived my whole life for you."
>
> Gary's life had suddenly become quite complicated. A short while ago it had all seemed so easy. "Even the kids were on Joanne's side," he muttered. Starting a new life was going to be hard.

Men react to divorce in various ways. Some find a new woman. In many cases, they found the new woman before the divorce. Others may withdraw from life or pretend that they are younger and single again. Sometimes they try to experience ten years in one. For many, relationships that follow a divorce appear superficial. It is difficult being happy with someone after having shared life and intimacy with a spouse. Men typically like to feel that they are being taken care of, and after divorce many feel that no one cares anymore. Questions about their children keep haunting them, too. "How do I reach the kids?" Although their father is experiencing new things and changing, the children want the same old dad. But that man is gone.

> At first, Larry wanted to be everything for his children. "But then I got tired of being super-dad," he said. "All the presents and the movies. I got out of my relationship because I wanted to be real. I figured if my children didn't like me for what I was, or rather what I was becoming, the hell with it."

Traditionally, males are taught to be providers and supporters. In the career world, they are looked at as the decision makers. After divorce, they are keeping house, eating out, making their own meals, and forced to leave the home they worked so hard to buy. All the things a man may have wanted are taken away and there is little to fill the gap.

> Jack had nightmares and thought that he was going crazy. "I still dream about wanting to kill her," he said. "I'm so angry about her finding someone else and kicking me out of my own house. She acts as if I'm some terrible disease. I still can't understand what happened. I know that we were having problems, but she never shared with me how she was feeling. I just feel like my whole world is a whirlwind. I can't seem to make sense of this."

Chapter 2 — Coping with Divorce

It is clear that both women and men who suffer through divorce come to their next marriages with much emotional baggage. So how do these two new types of people unite, as is the case of the stepfamily? The single woman with children is looking for a new relationship with equality, seeking a man who is accepting of her new career and willing to love her children as much as he loves her. As for the men, many are confused about their roles. They still want to be taken care of but realize that their roles and the roles of divorced women have changed. They want to be supportive of their new wives, but many do not know how.

They have little experience at marriage with this different kind of woman.

Both men and women must cope with the expectations, desires, past messages, failures, needs for security, children and relatives that come with their new families. Where does it all begin and end? Relationships will never be the same for these people. Once divorced, always cautious. All the people who seemed to be a part of the divorced man or woman's life—boyfriends, girlfriends, ex-spouses, children, parents, and friends—are different. It can be a most confusing and frightening period.

The man and woman want to be sure that they are not making another mistake and they realize that the odds are even higher this time. Yet finding someone and falling in love may prove to be a greater hassle than anticipated. Just because they have started a new relationship does not mean that the divorce is over and can be forgotten. Many aspects of it will continue to arise.

Getting one's life together after a divorce is a tremendous task. Some people never quite make it and continue to live in their pasts. Others decide that life is worth the struggle and they move ahead, leaving the remnants of the former relationships behind.

Chapter 3
Beginning New Relationships

Love is an exciting word. It conjures exciting and intoxicating images for many of us. Yet it is a word with many meanings. The meaning of love for a sixteen-year-old is quite different than what it is for a mature adult. Sometimes infatuation is mistaken for love, but it is difficult to separate the two. The emotions of a person who is infatuated with another may be just as strong as those of a person in love. Infatuation, however, fades quickly whereas love, when nurtured, deepens and grows. In this chapter we will look at the process of love from the perspective of the divorced person with children and the potential stepfamily member.

After getting a divorce, most people do not know how they feel about themselves or the opposite sex. Most have been rejected by the ex-spouse in numerous ways, and may have developed hangups about their looks, their sexuality, their skill to carry on an interesting conversation, and their ability to manage their lives effectively— in short, they may lose confidence and come to question their self- worth.

Unable to confront his feelings after his divorce, Greg found that the easiest way to cope was to work. "I had worked my way to the top by practically living my job. Besides all the nights and all I traveled, I brought work home with me. It was usually the weekend that upset Sherry the most. If we had a free night, I'd always entertain clients or stay home and sleep. She got tired of the whole grind and felt bored. I tried to change, but I was afraid I'd lose my job or be stuck where I was. So finally she left and I was really at a loss. I didn't know what to do. Maybe I should have taken some time for myself but the pain was too much. Instead I kept spending time at the job, even more than before. Going home was lonely and I tried to be there as little as possible. But you know, even in all my work I felt a piece of me was missing. I still was so damn lonely. Finally I figured out that the problem was me, and that it wouldn't be solved unless I took a good look at myself and my life."

Not everyone who attempts to hide from his or her problems turns to work. Some get invested in their children's lives and spend much of their time at children's activities. Others may immerse themselves in community projects. Some may think of members of the opposite sex as being worthless, and so they spend their time avoiding potential partners. Eventually, however, all types of avoidance wear thin.

The underlying problem is simple. Once we have experienced a deep relationship and have known love (no matter how short it may have been), it is tough to forget and live without. Life is more exciting and worthwhile when shared with someone who understands us. And so, generally, we lick our wounds and recover. For some it may take six months, for some six years, but most of us do recover. When we do, we go searching for that special someone. We believe that this time it will be different. This time that special person will be just right. This time, he or she will look great, talk with intelligence, listen attentively, and satisfy our every need.

That is how it usually goes—initially. It is after marriage that life begins to change. The "institution" brings people to their senses. We have discovered that many couples believe that this infatuation stage should last forever. But that is impossible. As the actor Roy Schneider stated once in an interview, "If I stayed like I am when I first fell in love, I'd never get a damn thing done

Chapter 3   Beginning New Relationships

in life." Falling in love is a great experience, but that feeling does not last forever. With time, and with the right person, it changes into deeper, more profound emotions. With the wrong person, it changes, too, but in this case the changes are unpleasant.

For those looking for someone to love, the process is difficult. Searching for a potential partner at the job, cocktail parties, social organizations, or even at singles bars is a hazardous and uncertain undertaking. Most people get angry and frustrated, as they soon learn that single life is not all it is supposed to be for the divorced person. After all, there is a major difference between the divorced single and other singles. The divorced single has been in love before. Having progressed for years into an intimate relationship, the divorced single has experienced both the good and the bad.

It often happens that after a husband and wife divorce, for a time, they may remain attracted to each other even if they are extremely angry. Some of that comes from the closeness of finally being able to communicate. Once outside the bounds of marriage, conversations may become more open and friendly. Discussions may be over the children, the furniture, or the admitting that it is finally over, but a couple often learns to share. Unfortunately, coming at this stage, the ability to share comes too late.

Ann found that parting was the most difficult thing she had ever done. "Saying goodbye to Dennis just tore me up. It took me years to get up the courage to tell him that it was over. The funny thing was that it really didn't take either of us by surprise. We both knew that our relationship hadn't been good for either one of us. But asking someone to walk out the door and seeing the person actually going are two different things. I felt like the biggest creep in the world. I still love him but I just can't live with him. We each do too much damage."

Most of us have fond memories of our old car, and the same is true of past relationships. In time, hopefully, the pain and hurt diminish. One remembers the good things and the attempts made to save the marriage. Sometimes the memories are bitter, but most often they are tinged with regret. Many people ask themselves, "What did I do wrong? Couldn't we have made it?" Songwriters know our hearts and write lyrics that paint these images. Yet out of the sadness of ended relationships also comes anger.

In therapy, John did not know what to do with his rage. "It seems like I'm mad at everybody; my boss, my secretary, and my kids. The funny thing is, I can't be mad at her. When I talk to her I just feel this emptiness in my stomach. It's overwhelming. Life without her means nothing to me. How could she end our marriage? I just don't understand what happened?"

After touching and being touched, it is difficult to live without intimacy. After being married, it is often painful to live without the former spouse even though the marriage may have been failing long before the divorce became final.

If there is ever a resounding melody after a marriage, it is loneliness. Sometimes it gets in the way of making clear decisions. It is easy to forget the past relationship and how things must change if they are to be better the second time. It is not uncommon for people to view their former marriage with such nostalgia that they end up marrying someone just like their former spouses. This usually leads to trouble and failure. Finding someone to fill the gaps caused by loneliness is easy; finding someone to love is not.

Susan fell into this trap. "I felt so lonely that I dated Bob out of my need for someone. It sounds crazy, but I wanted my independence and yet I couldn't stand to be alone. When I married Bob, I found that I was reliving my first marriage in a matter of months. I was reliving all the same hassles and problems. It was like a recurring nightmare."

To compound the problem, most people change over time. This is especially true after experiencing an event like divorce. Before finding another mate, people must re-evaluate their priorities. They must become reacquainted with themselves before they can find someone who can satisfy their needs. Following are several questions that must be considered:

- Is work important to me? If yes, how much?
- What is important to me in life?
- What do I feel sexually?
- What are my priorities?
- What kind of partner would I be happy with?
- What are the roles I want in a relationship?
- What type of relationship do I want?
- What are some important rules I have in relationships?

- Do I want to be free or controlled?
- Do I wish to travel more?
- Do I want to buy the things I have always wanted to buy?
- Will I try to be less or more serious about life?

There are, of course, still other questions that each individual must pose to himself or herself. Divorce can be a very introspective process. At the least, it demands that individuals re-examine themselves and face what they may have been avoiding for years.

After Divorce for the Woman

Sexuality can be a difficult issue for both men and women, but frequently the greatest burden falls on women. Inadequate sexual practices play a part in many divorces, and each spouse usually blames the other.

Diane thought Jon was too macho. "He just is in it for himself," she said. "Whenever he wants sex, I'm supposed to cry for joy. Well, it just doesn't seem fun for me."

On the other hand, Peter feels neglected. "It's like I have to beg for sex. If I behave a certain way and I do what she wants, I get rewarded. I feel like I'm a dog who begs for a bone."

Although both partners are usually responsible for sexual problems in a marriage, in our society the woman usually gets the blame. She is labeled as frigid, non- orgasmic, or just does not know how to "turn on" a man. Some women become so concerned about their supposed sexual inadequacy that they venture to consult sex therapists without examining their past partner's role in intimate relations.

Cindy thought that she was a sexual misfit until she got divorced. "I thought sex was something that you had to do. All those wondrous magazines talked about orgasm as if it was like eating ice cream. Everybody does it. Well, I guess I wasn't everybody. Fred just got his kicks and it was over in a few minutes. When I asked him to get some therapy with me, he said it was my problem. In a way, he was right. My problem was him. After I got divorced, Tim showed me that I wasn't crazy. Sex could be both fun and caring. It was like opening a whole new world for me. I may not have 50 orgasms a day, but I feel close to someone when I go to bed."

Despite the labels and accusations, the sexual activity of many couples in the later stages of a marriage is rather dismal. It is not uncommon for therapists to hear couples admit that they have not experienced intercourse on a regular basis for several months and sometimes years. In marriage counseling, we rarely see a couple who have a troubled marriage but are sharing a vibrant sexual relationship.

When a marriage ends, the man and woman may have many doubts about sex and future partners. Sometimes, these doubts are for good reasons. Newly divorced people, having been married for quite some time, may feel uncomfortable dating again. Life has suddenly, and quite radically, changed.

"I feel out of place here," states Jack, a 42-year-old business executive. "I never was very good with giggling girls. I'm looking for someone who's mature. I'm not looking for a sexual relationship. I'm looking for a relationship. I need someone to care for me."

Some of the self-doubts arise from other reasons. Someone who had an inadequate sexual partner may not know what a good sexual relationship is. Most of us have not had that many encounters. If you have had sex with ten people before you married, that is several times more than for many women and men. The person who has been told that he or she is lousy in bed may be reluctant to experience sexual relations with a new partner.

Consider the case of Suzanne. She was married for ten years to a singer in a local band, but was becoming tired of the routine into which her marriage had fallen. Sex was a major problem. In the beginning, her sexual relationship with her husband was great, but it began to deteriorate once they started having problems in their marriage. During the last year of their marriage, they seldom had sex. Her husband, Joe, says, "She's an awful lover and frigid." Suzanne says, "He's in a hurry and exceedingly horny."

After their divorce, Suzanne saw a therapist and tried to understand what had gone wrong. At first she tried to avoid the topic of sexuality, but eventually she revealed her doubts

Chapter 3 — Beginning New Relationships

> *in humorous undertones. After being in therapy for several months, she met a sensitive man who invited her for a weekend rendezvous. To test him on the first night, she rejected his advances. With quiet understanding, he accepted her choice. On the second night, Suzanne agreed and experienced sex that was satisfying and ego-strengthening. She began to realize that poor relationships make for poor sex, and that caring sex is a process that involves two people and not just one. Suzanne had been blaming herself for the sexual problems in her marriage when in fact the problem was shared by her husband as well.*

The sexual game can be played in still other fashions. Some women may use sex as a weapon within the relationship, employing a type of "if you're nice, you'll get some" ultimatum. Unfortunately, it is easy to lose track of the game and forget how to love. People caught in such relationships inevitably find themselves frightened and frustrated.

Still other women may hide sexual insecurities by acting as if they are the virtuous virgin who has never experienced sex or slept with a man.

> *Jackie was an example of this type of woman. Invited for a weekend by an older and established businessman, she pretends that she does not know what might occur. She brings two sets of clothes (sexy and virginal) and dares not discuss the nature of the weekend. Most assuredly she will torment the man to all extremes, and eventually may submit her newfound virginity in a lost moment of ignorance while intoxicated. In the morning she will feign all knowledge of the incident and regret having ever done it. Jackie's actions help her to ignore the realities of being an older woman and divorced.*

Today the media often trumpets the casualness of sex, particularly with the realistic fear of AIDS. Casual sex has severe complications in today's world. However, when sex involves love, commitment and caring, these are what make sex and intimacy fulfilling. It takes honest, introspective people to recognize this process.

After Divorce for the Man

Women like Jackie are just part of the dilemma for the man after divorce. The man's journey of insecurity is threatening. No longer does he have youth, yet he must compete against a younger, fitter image of himself. He, too, may question his sexuality. Probably, for years, he has wondered if he is sexually okay and desirable to another woman. Most men look for a partner whom they perceive as being less or equal to themselves and rarely do they set goals for the unattainable.

Ted illustrates this tendency. "I have a strong need to be boss and so I keep picking dependent type of women. A woman who is strong is scary to me and not worth the hassle. When I pick someone dependent, she usually gets too clingy and I want to leave. On the other hand, an independent woman resents my bossiness and ends up telling me to get lost. I've been working on changing my perspective but it is hard."

Thus the man debates about his "perfect" partner: the slim, trim, vivacious woman that he always desired. Too often, this image is unrealistic.

Divorce alters the man's former lifestyle quite dramatically. Used to having had many things done for him, suddenly he must shop, clean, launder his clothes, and make his own meals (or eat out). Most men dislike doing all this, and look for someone to take care of them. Of any group, men who had the most rigid and conservative sex role patterns in their marriages have the most difficulty coping with their divorces.

Men also deal with the concept of failure in a marriage differently than women do. They focus much energy on career goals, but most successful career men benefit from having supportive women behind them. The myth that "behind every successful man is a woman" is not all myth. Most men work best and achieve the most success on the job when they enjoy a settled home life. Substituting work for a lover, however, grates on the emotional psyche.

Frequently, men are more reluctant in establishing a new relationship than women. It is typical for the man to lose out financially in divorce, and some men simply cannot afford to get married again. Furthermore, the scars of losing a relationship

Chapter 3 — Beginning New Relationships

can be deep, especially since many men project feelings inward and have difficulty releasing guilt and hostility. This leads to the feeling that all women are bad, and fosters the fear of rejection.

Sometimes this feeling is behind the man who becomes "macho" and uses women for whatever he can get. Rather than face his feelings, the macho man puts up an impenetrable wall and sees relationships as endless sexual encounters. Trapped in his bitterness, he begins to run out of prospects as his partners realize his selfish needs.

Like women, most men are hurt by divorce. In many ways they react to the experience differently, yet, like women, they must be willing to examine the past, find the causes for the failure of their marriages, and work to build new lives with satisfying relationships.

A Final Mate

If men and women can overcome their doubts and try again, romance can be fulfilling. Relationships the second time around usually progress faster and to a deeper level because partners seek intimacy. The relationship may have a mature note, particularly if children are involved. While children should be a part of the relationship, they should not be the major part.

The initial focus of any relationship should be on the couple, and how they can realize enjoyment and build happy memories. That is why the beginning of the relationship is so exciting. You feel happy, silly, confused, and madly in love. Your lover is constantly on your mind, and the two of you are always arranging to meet. Life is a whirlpool of thoughts and it is difficult to focus on anything else. Even money does not seem to matter! When we look at relationships, we call this the ecstasy or first stage of intimacy. It can last from a month to six months or a year.

The second, or realistic, stage begins a period of change for the couple. They begin to feel serious about the relationship and start contemplating its future. Romance is still alive and well, but money is now considered and discussed. Questions like: "Who pays?" and "Can we afford to do that?" are raised. This is the period where the couple test each other to see if each person is fully committed to the relationship. This stage is usually shorter than the first.

The last, or commitment, stage is where a couple finally decides that the relationship is very serious and worthy of consideration for marriage. With the stepfamily, crucial topics and agendas are now discussed, as is often the case with a "first time" marrying couple.

Usually both people, or at least one, have been in a relationship before, and they have an idea of what can go wrong. With a stepfamily, however, they usually discuss surface matters and are afraid to deal with the real issues. After all, the future spouse may pull out if the marriage appears that it might be hard. Children will be involved, too, and this will bring both considerable happiness and problems for the remarrying couple.

Once remarried, each spouse will attempt to relive past marriages and discuss how things "were," or how things "weren't," with an ex-spouse. While this can have some value, it can also create resentment and jealousy. The new couple needs to set their own course and to forget as much of the past as possible. There will be enough haunting memories and they do not need to create more.

A successful remarriage is built on far more than just luck. It takes honesty, good communication, a willingness to face reality, and, perhaps most importantly, a willingness to compromise.

Chapter 4
Preparing for Remarriage

Why do people want to get married when they have already failed once in the process and now have children to complicate the problems? After all, the odds of a first marriage making it in America are about fifty-fifty. The odds for remarriage are worse.

For most divorced men and women, living as a single person is a temporary stage in life. Most divorced persons remarry within five years after their divorce. About two out of five people who divorced in the last decade will remarry and many others will have a cohabitational relationship.

From these numbers it is clear that marriage has considerable value in our culture and society. Marriage is a form of commitment and bonding that most people view as a permanent proposition. People do not enter into marriage expecting it to fail. Remarriage is just as attractive to divorced persons as it is for the single, never-married.

Step by Step: A Guide to Stepfamily Living

The desire for remarriage in our culture has not changed much since colonial days. In the past people remarried after the death of a spouse because they needed a partner to help them survive the harsh environment. Today remarriage can improve financial conditions, end loneliness and isolation, offer contact with new friends or couples, make one "normal" to peers, and provide a parent to children.

Of course, making a second marriage work is no less difficult than insuring that a first marriage is successful. For a remarriage that leads to the formation of a stepfamily, the commitment needs to be even stronger than the commitment for the first marriage. The new husband and wife must cope not only with their needs, but with the needs of children. This is a high-risk process.

Unfortunately, most couples do not know how to prepare for remarriage and the formation of a stepfamily. When problems arise, which they inevitably do, they often seem to be bigger and more pressing than in the previous marriage. No one wants to fail, but no one knows what to do. The members of the stepfamily have no models, no experience for what they are facing. What worked in the first marriage often does not work in the stepfamily. In our research and clinical practice we have discovered that it takes nearly two years for family members in a remarriage to become comfortable in their new roles. We have found this to generally be true, based on experiences in our own family, as well as on the experiences of the families we have counseled. This time of solidifying the new family is a period of misery and joy. It is also an opportunity for personal growth.

Examining the potential problems before remarriage can help a couple in their efforts to make their marriage successful. When we work with remarried couples, we consistently find five areas that are potential sticks of dynamite: money, rules and roles, children, sex and intimacy, and parents.

The Issue of Money

To many individuals, money means freedom. Money enables people to choose the way they want to live. It offers the ability to buy the necessities and luxuries of life. Yet money can also become a battleground for a couple.

Consider the example of Sallie, a single parent. Although she has decided to remarry, she has serious reservations which she has failed to discuss with her future husband. Sallie has been the head of her household, and, though she likes the financial security a husband's income will provide, she has no intention of surrendering control of her money. She hesitates to include her savings into a joint account because she has saved more than he has. Sallie would also like to maintain her own checking account, and believes that she is more competent at handling money than her future mate. She feels strongly about all this, primarily because her first husband left her with nothing.

Her future husband Harry, however, is just as adamant in his opinions about money. Stung for a sizable loss in his first marriage, he has promised himself that he will "do it right this time." While he is quite willing to provide nice comforts for everyone, he will sign all the checks and will maintain control over his earnings. He intends to have both joint accounts with Sallie, and separate accounts for himself. Convinced that he is the better money-manager, Harry expects Sallie to turn her resources over to him.

Clearly, Sallie and Harry are heading for trouble. Money is an important part of the modern relationship, but when it becomes the focal point in a marriage it can discolor everything else.

The key to keeping money in its proper place in a marriage is negotiation and compromise. Money can take on great significance in remarriages. The new husband and wife have both worked hard for some security and neither wants to see the results of that work lost. First-marrieds usually form their ideas about money and the marriage together. Remarrieds come to the new marriage with their ideas about money already formed. Discussing the issue of money honestly before remarriage can help couples share their views and arrive at compromise.

Perhaps most importantly, a couple considering remarriage should examine past practices and the problems they experience over money in their previous marriages. What was the relationship over money with their previous spouses? Who did what and why? Was the former husband or wife a big spender? Was the former husband or wife a good manager of money? A poor one? The new couple should also examine their financial roles in the prior marriages. What were their strengths and weaknesses in the handling of money? What are their feelings about money now?

They should also discuss their present assets and what each individual will bring to the relationship. After all, it is a partnership. If necessary, a legal contract outlining what belongs to each should be written by an attorney. This may protect partners should the marriage falter.

Along with sharing ideas and feelings about money, a couple should evaluate financial sex roles. In most couples today, both the husband and wife work. Men who can provide for their families and prefer that their wives remain at home must share their feelings with their prospective wives. Likewise, women who have careers and do not wish to give them up must tell their future husbands. Furthermore, couples must decide whether they will maintain joint accounts or separate ones, who will write out the checks, and how the money will be spent.

Closely related to money are questions and problems about material possessions. Since partners who are remarrying usually come to the new marriage with many material possessions, concerns over which to keep and which to discard can become major dilemmas. Arguments over furniture, for example, are not uncommon.

Lou is a good example. He did not like sitting in his living room, because half of the furniture reminded him of his past life with his ex-wife while the other half reminded him of his children and his new wife. Instead of relaxing, he found sitting in the room to be unpleasant. To solve the problem, Lou and his wife agreed to buy new furniture. In throwing out the old, Lou also threw out old memories. To Lou, investing in new furniture was investing in his new family.

Children can be another source of financial problems. Couples must discuss how much money they are willing to spend on the children. This becomes especially important if both man and woman come to the new marriage with their own children. Will spending be equal for all the children? Will more be spent on the older ones? What about child support? If child support is not enough, is the new spouse willing to contribute to that child's welfare?

Money has the potential to split a new marriage apart. It should never be put between a couple, but should be discussed openly and honestly. A couple must come to an agreement about money management, or money will become a constant battle that will undermine the marriage.

Rules and Roles

Sex roles have changed dramatically in the last decade. Both men and women are more confused than ever about what their roles are. Although the battle for equal rights is often beamed into our homes via the evening news on TV, the biggest equal rights battles are within the home itself. With both parents working, most women are tired of working at a full-time job plus keeping the house clean, doing laundry, raising the children, and cooking. Most men are starting to give some help (some more reluctantly than others), and will be expected to give even more in the future.

The couple that marries without fully discussing sex roles is heading for trouble. Partners need to agree on who does what, where and when. We frequently tell couples, "The less you talk, the more angry you'll get." Some of the areas that should be discussed in detail are meal cooking, household chores, shopping, yard work, car repairs, cleaning, clothes washing, ironing, dish washing , and home repairs.

Some couples find that they feel most comfortable with a written contract detailing responsibilities. Others feel that a simple agreement is good enough. While compromise is vital, a fair division of chores is based on common sense. Sharon and Phil, for example, had all of the household tasks split up so that even their sweat was divided equally. They set up a schedule and put it on their home computer. Unfortunately, they soon began to feel so regimented that they felt they were in the army.

Equality is certainly an appropriate goal, but one that is difficult to reach. We have found that the best marriages have partners that work together and help each other frequently and lovingly. They transcend equality into mutuality.

Children

Many people, as they blissfully saunter to remarriage, forget to consider their children and are surprised by the tornado that later rampages through their lives. Aside from how money will be spent on the children, basic questions about upbringing and parenting must be considered. What will the rules for the children be, and who will enforce them? Other typical questions: What will the children call the stepparent? What last name will the children use? Should they be involved in helping plan or participate in the wedding? How do the parents get time away from the children?

When working with parents, we set rules that help families function. We assume that the parents are "in charge" and will provide adequate role models. For example, we believe it is helpful if the stepparent is called Mom or Dad whenever feasible. This may not be immediately accepted by the children, but it is important in achieving closeness in the family. Words create intimacy as well as distance in relationships. After all, stepparents often do what mothers and fathers do, and they deserve the honor of the title. Moreover, giving them that title helps the stepparent and children to become committed to each other. We emphasize this even if the stepparent feels uncomfortable or is reluctant to build a relationship with the children. We have found that if the stepparent has the title, he or she usually acts the part.

Some of our colleagues disagree with us on this, but we believe it is helpful in most families. Often the members of the new stepfamily do not want to commit to being a family and resist that vital sense of belonging. They let the old rules get in the way of their love. Some therapists unwittingly contribute to the problem. Because they only believe in the traditional family, they counsel that the new family should strive to achieve and maintain traditional roles. Phrases like, "Remember, there's only one Mom or Dad," permeates the counseling session, but such counsel hinders rather than helps a stepfamily.

Step by Step: A Guide to Stepfamily Living

When we work with families, our thinking runs counter to the old philosophy. If a stepparent assumes the role of a mother or father, he or she deserves to be called Mom or Dad. The only instances in which we do not insist on this are when a child sees a stepparent infrequently, if an adolescent is ready to leave the family, or if the family feels very uncomfortable with the title and needs more time to adjust to the new relationships they are experiencing.

Parents should set the guidelines for appropriate behaviors and take the lead in the family. One of their first decisions that can set the tone regards the last name the children will use. Last names are often a major hassle and legal triangle. It is unfortunate that our legal system permits children to have different last names than those of their parents. These children are immediately identified as being different. The introduction goes something like this: "Hi, I'm Sam Jones and this is my son, Joe. No, Joe Smith, not Joe Jones. He's mine, but not really. Well, I just pay the bills." We suggest that whenever possible, and if everyone agrees, the members of stepfamilies should have the same last name. It is psychologically healthier for the custodial parent and the children to have the same last name. This particularly supports the identity of the child and the parent since the majority of custodial parents are women. It is also less "sex discriminating" because this last name issue is based solely on the need of the male adult and not for the child.

The identity of the children is also aided by each child having a room or space within the new home or apartment. This space should be planned beforehand, and discussed as if everyone was moving into a new house, even if all of the family members are not new.

A feeling of belonging and sense of family is essential for all members of the stepfamily. This is why the children should be involved in the wedding ceremony, whether or not they want to be. Pouting and crying should be discouraged through proper discipline and discussion. Angry adolescents can learn that loving a parent means opening their hearts and minds to others. The wedding symbolizes the birth of the new family, and everyone should be involved.

Chapter 4   Preparing for Remarriage

Sex and Intimacy

Many couples find that sex is better before marriage; after marriage it disappears along with the romance. To prevent a big letdown in their sexual relations, we encourage couples to be open and honest about their sexual expectations before they get married.

While taking time out for romance is important, avoiding the sexual shortcomings of the previous marriages may be more vital. Remarrieds often set up the new spouse as a perfect sex-mate. This person is expected to do everything right where the former spouse did everything wrong. When the new spouse does not live up to these expectations, disappointment and disillusion arise.

A long discussion about sexual needs before marriage can help prevent some problems and eliminate others. If a couple is having sexual problems before marriage, they will likely continue having the same problems after taking their wedding vows. Such couples should consider seeing a marriage counselor who is knowledgeable in sex therapy.

Since an inadequate sexual relationship is often a symptom that something else is going wrong in a marriage, a man and woman need to be frank and look for the problems. They must discuss what is happening in their relationship, not what is occurring in the bedroom. People often hide problems in the hope that they will solve themselves. This seldom happens. Problems in a relationship need to be confronted and resolved mutually. Couples who can talk about problems and share their feelings before marriage are off to a good start toward intimacy. Couples who have trouble talking about problems prior to marrying will most assuredly have more problems afterward.

In counseling couples we have found that sex is often an unspoken or forbidden topic. It is a subject that is difficult to discuss and problems associated with it are usually put off or brushed aside. Unfortunately, unless faced and resolved, sexual problems can become major barriers to a couple's relationship.

Parents

Parental involvement— one's own parents as well as future in-laws— may also be an obstacle for a couple beginning a stepfamily. It is often true that the first wedding is for one's parents and not really for the couple. The second time around can be quite different. The parents of a couple who wish to remarry may not approve of the marriage, and they can bring considerable pressure on the couple.

There are many reasons for this response. The parents may be overprotective. They do not want to see their child hurt again. No matter how good the intended spouse is, he or she is not good enough.

The parents may find it hard to break off with the former son-in-law or daughter-in-law. They may find it hard to understand how their son or daughter could divorce such a good mate. They may find it horrible that the children will have a new parent.

Some parents cannot accept that their child has divorced. That of itself is terrible, and remarriage in their eyes is worse. Some parents simply do not believe in divorce or remarriage.

Parents may also be afraid of change. This is especially true if they are dependent on the child, or if the child is still dependent on them. They may feel threatened by the idea of remarriage because they think it will mean loss of the child's love.

Finally, parents may find it difficult to build a relationship with the new spouse. The ordinary conventions do not apply. Usually there is no asking for the daughter's hand. Parents of the spouses do not need to meet. The marriage may be a small one. Children may or may not be involved. Relatives may feel uncomfortable.

Even though they may be feeling some or all of these concerns, many parents take a wait-and-see attitude toward remarriage and the stepfamily. However, this can anger the couple because parental acceptance is one of the keys in life to feeling good about oneself. Complicating the matter is the realization by most remarrying couples, that they have their own lives and happiness to consider with or without the approval of their parents. Some parents attempt to make their children choose between themselves and remarrying. They may not say this outright, but their treatment of the prospective spouse and their comments about him or her send very clear signals. The choice can be a hard one.

In some cases, relations become strained and a couple do not invite their parents to a remarriage ceremony. This often results in a hurt that takes a long time to heal. Furthermore, because their parents were not at the ceremony, the marriage may lack a sense of legitimacy.

Communication is essential to avoid parental problems. Every attempt should be made to discuss the concerns of parents. They need to understand the couple's feelings, as well as their own. Stepfamilies are difficult adventures that fare better with the support of all family members.

The Honeymoon

Many couples who remarry do not go on a honeymoon. After the ceremony they step right into the home and family. We feel that this is a mistake.

Taking a honeymoon, even for a day, shows the children and everyone else that the husband and wife are in love. If a honeymoon at a hotel is not affordable, a couple should consider sending the children away and having a honeymoon at the home for a few days. Having some time alone at the beginning of the marriage is important. It gives the couple a chance to set up the house, do some redecorating (this is essential if the home is the home of one of the partners and the former spouse lived there), and make the home more like "ours" rather than his or hers. When the children return, make sure that they have their own rooms or space. Everyone must have a place in the new family.

It is crucial that the parents demonstrate that they both belong and will be contributors to the family. Children may not agree with this, but it is the way it must be.

Marriage is a major commitment. This is true whether one is getting married for the first time or second time. Sharing feelings and expectations can help make the transition to marriage smoother and insure the strength of the marriage.

Chapter 5
The Role of Children When a Couple Decides to Remarry

Falling in love is one of the most exciting things that happens to people. It is a time of high energy, a time when the world and each day seem worthwhile. Eventually that initial excitement fades, but hopefully it is replaced by a deeper love.

In trying to find that deeper love, people often focus on the good things of their relationship and ignore the problems. They want the good things to continue; they do not want to upset the relationship.

This is particularly true of people who are considering remarriage. Many of the people who are planning to remarry are still trying to accept their divorces and are still in mourning. Yet here they are thinking about starting a new family. They are trying to build a new relationship. They are falling in love and want that love to grow and deepen.

With all these changes, it is not hard to see that when children are involved, they are not the top priority in their parents' lives. The parent may say to himself or herself that the children still are number one, but it is the parent and not the children who is falling in love. It is the parent who is experiencing the highs and lows of intimacy. Most children have trouble understanding what is occurring. They do not have the same concept of love that adults have. They are not grown-up and their concepts are young and not developed. Adults know that love can be an enriching experience, but it involves much more than fairy tale romance.

That understanding of the complexity and power of love is why adults play games with it. Most of the time, they are scared. They are afraid that their partners will not like parts of them, or they are fearful of making the commitment that love demands.

For many couples who are starting a stepfamily, children present a major problem. To avoid it, or at least prevent it from growing beyond control, couples should work to help their children understand the process. Marriage in a stepfamily is a package deal and one cannot separate the contents. However, it is helpful to remember that children grow up and eventually leave. The person who stays behind, the mate, should be the focus of the marriage from the other partner's viewpoint. Sometimes that is difficult to understand.

We recall one client who was thinking about divorce for five years, but could not bring herself to leave her husband. She stayed because of her children. Every time she decided to leave, her parents and friends would say, "You can't leave your children." This woman went through marital, family, and individual therapy. She talked until she had no words left. One day she quietly came into our office and said, "You know, living with someone you don't love is like being in a prison cell. I'm sentenced to boredom and hostility. My kids are going to grow up, leave me, and be okay. I can't wait around ten years for them to leave. It isn't fair." She finally made a choice and left.

Just like choosing a partner, choosing to keep the husband and wife as the primary focus of the family is vital. We believe that stepfamilies fail because marital relationships fail. Children should never get in the way of a marriage. Even when life with children is terrible, it is essential that a couple keep loving each other. That love is the foundation for the family. If the foundation remains strong, other problems have a chance to be resolved. If the husband and wife continue to love each other, the children will often feel more secure and the family will develop a stronger identity.

Chapter 5　　　　　　The Role of Children in the Remarriage

Without question, single parents wanting to start a stepfamily have a tough time. Most custodial single parents are women, and this is usually prescribed by law. This is changing, but the change is slow as judges are reluctant to separate children from their mothers, even when they are delinquent parents. Sadly, many female single parents have been abandoned by their husbands and have incomes below the poverty level.

Finding a man who is willing to marry a woman with children is difficult. However, the chances against finding a man become even greater when a woman makes her children the first and only priority in her life. Likewise, the man who makes his children the most important and only people in his life will have trouble building a solid relationship with a woman.

A couple contemplating remarriage must work on developing a romance. Time alone, candlelight dinners, or occasional weekends away are crucial to building the foundation of the relationship and giving love a chance to grow. While the length of time each couple needs for this varies, they should have a good understanding of each other before the children become involved.

The time spent together should be a time for communication and sharing. A man and woman should discuss their life together, their expectations, goals, attitudes, values, and, of course, their families. All parties will need time for adjustment, but a strong beginning will eliminate many problems later.

While children should get to know their parent's future spouse, they should not be allowed to intrude upon the developing relationship. A parent should avoid siding with his or her children against the future spouse. The man and woman will be seeking intimacy; they will understand each other best and should always keep each other in mind. Children will respect parents who place their marriage first. The children are important, but not as important as the love between husband and wife because it is that love that provides the foundation for the family.

The time during which a couple is dating can be explosive for children. For example, adolescents will often express their opinions. Jealousy will be manifest. The words can be harsh:

"How dare you spend time with him when you should spend time with me?"

"You went to that place without me? You know I wanted to go."

"You do all the fun things with her."

Sometimes their comments can be blunt as well as painful:

"I think he's a creep."

"She's really ugly. How can you go out with her?"

Children can also be remarkably adept at playing with a parent's guilt. The following remarks are typical:

"Are you going to bed with him?"

"He's not like Daddy."

"I can't talk to her like I could with Mom."

The comments of children may sound cruel, but that is only because the children are confused and hurt. They do not understand their feelings, or what is happening to their parents.

Children are not adults, and cannot be expected to behave as adults. Developmentally, children are self-centered, selfish and immature. They believe the world is just for them and that they deserve everything. Children need to learn to be adults and must practice loving and sharing, and parents must be their teachers and role models.

In our practice, we have seen this repeatedly in stepfamilies. Conversations like the following are quite common:

Child: You mean you're serious. She's awful!

Father: Well, she was okay a week ago. You said you liked her then.

Child: Yeah, but you didn't love her then. I don't really like her.

Father: What don't you like about her? *(The father is asking for trouble here.)*

Child: Well, she's too bossy. She's not like Mom is, and she never pays enough attention to me. She's always talking to you.

Father: She likes you. She thinks you're great.

Child: Yeah, well I don't like her.

Chapter 5 The Role of Children in the Remarriage

From this point the conversation usually escalates into an argument, until the child explodes and stomps from the room.

Adults may not understand the insecurities and resentment that occur during this time for children.

For instance, whenever Sally has her steady over, her Johnny sits between them. Asking him to move is hopeless. When he is put to bed, he screams and yells until Sally's friend leaves. Johnny is doing his best to keep his mother to himself. While Susie's tactics are different—she drinks scalding hot tea, screams, and falls down— her purpose is the same. She wants all of her father's attention when he is entertaining a potential mate. Susie wants to be the only female in her father's life, and she will do whatever is necessary to insure that position.

Certainly not all children refuse to accept a new Mom or Dad, but for most families the children's acceptance is a difficult point. The matter is worsened when adults have trouble managing the children. Sometimes, hopeful of winning the children over, the new parent gives them gifts. This is nothing more than a type of bribery and seldom works. Gift-giving is not the way to build good relationships. Time spent with the children is much better than the giving of any material object. Relationships cannot be bought.

Gaining the confidence and love of the children is not easy for a stepparent. The mate must be reassuring and helpful, for there will be times when the future spouse may be driven to extreme frustration. There may even be fireworks.

When he and Darlene were dating, Bob, who had little previous experience with children, was at a loss how to cope with her five-year-old son. Exploding one day, he spanked the boy.

"I felt so embarrassed that it happened," he softly related later. "Joey just kept pushing me, was rude, and called me names. When he hit me out of anger, I set a limit and spanked him for his behavior. It was kind of crazy after that. Darlene stood up for me even though Joey cried up a storm and blamed me for being a mean person. But after that, he respected me and we are very close now."

As an adult and future stepparent, a person has to take a stand. Even if the children profess to hate the man or woman, respect must be insisted upon. Hostility must be controlled. When parents take charge of the situation from the beginning, the journey will be easier. Relationships take time to develop, but there is no reason family members cannot be treated civilly as relationships form.

There will be occasions when emotions get so strained that parents need to call a truce. Family members should be encouraged to sit down and share their feelings with each other openly and honestly. This can be difficult to do, but the benefits can be far-reaching. Courtesy, civility, and caring, which we call the Three C's, should be a part of every family.

From the Children's Viewpoint

While a man and woman should focus on each other during their dating, they also need to understand what is happening to their children. The children are suffering through as much insecurity and hurt as are the parents, but they do not have the experience of their parents to manage their emotions.

Most of the children who become members of stepfamilies have seen one parent leave. They have experienced hurt and loneliness. Many come to feel that they owe allegiance to their biological parents, and believe that it is betrayal to love someone else. Our culture puts a restriction on love; we do not have enough love in us to care for two mothers and fathers. The statement sounds silly, but people believe it. Moreover, relatives and friends reinforce the idea. Even if the biological parent is not as good to the children as the stepparent, the biological parent is still the only mother or father. Fighting this misconception can be hard, but it can be beaten through awareness and understanding. Children have an immense capacity for love. They can give much more than adults imagine.

Biological parents frequently compound the problems of the children. In many cases the biological parent is angry or jealous that the ex-spouse is getting married. The sharing of the children may seem in jeopardy, and the biological parent may fear being replaced by the stepparent. Since he or she is now part of the family, the stepparent assumes an important role in the life of the children, a condition that the biological parent may be unwilling to accept.

Chapter 5   The Role of Children in the Remarriage

The jealousy of the non-custodial, biological parent toward the stepparent may be exhibited in various ways, both subtle and overt. Comments such as, "He can never be your real Daddy," or "He's okay for a stepparent," are not uncommon. Sometimes children receive subtle messages of parental hurt or sorrow if they seem too happy or spend too much time with the stepparent. Remarks like, "He can never be as good as I am to you," are hard for children to forget, or understand. Another message we frequently hear is, "I'm so lonely without you."

As therapists we have found it frustrating when parents behave self-centeredly regarding their children, and thereby hurt them. In these situations children become possessions as one parent tries to outshine the other. The children become pawns in a game in which their perception of family can become distorted.

Unless the parent is an abuser, it does little good to cast that parent in an unfavorable light. The children will have a relationship and in this regard they have some say as to its depth. The arguments about who is a better parent lead nowhere.

Focus on the new family is paramount. No one can tell a husband and wife how to manage their family, though others will surely try. In the stepfamily, it is important for the husband and wife to be involved in the family as much as possible and let the other parent take responsibility for his or her actions. The more the ex-spouse is let into the stepfamily, even in a parenting role, the greater the problems the new couple will have in creating a new family.

It is important to note that, generally, a custodial parent will have the children most of the time. In this type of stepfamily, the stepparent will be able to have much contact and share many experiences with the children. Stepparents should take advantage of these times to build a strong relationship with the children.

The task of the custodial parent during the development of the relationship between children and future stepparent is twofold. While providing support for the new parent, he or she must also listen to the complaints of the children. Many children try to make the custodial parent divide allegiance between the stepparent and biological parent, creating a triangle of conflict. Our advice is for the custodial parent to stay out of this as much as possible, but if a choice must be made, it must be made in favor of the new spouse. The couple is starting a new family, and their allegiance must be to the new family.

This can be most difficult for the spouse who is still taking care of the former partner. Some people like to act married even after they are divorced. The facade helps reduce guilt. Sometimes, especially for nurturing types, taking care of the ex-spouse feels good. Eventually, however, a man and woman must choose the new spouse if the new family is to succeed.

Children will not fully trust the new parents until they are sure the couple is committed to each other. The children have too much to lose. Why get involved and give love if the marriage will not last? Children will not make the investment of love until they feel secure. That security must come from the married couple.

The Grandparents and the Children

While grandparents are quite happy to share their love with their grandchildren, they may not accept the idea of the stepfamily. For many parents of men and women who remarry and start stepfamilies, the divorce was at least comprehensible, but a stepfamily is simply too much to accept.

Parents of the custodial parent will often side with the other biological parent, even if they did not like that person throughout the marriage. They may also feel that the love of a stepparent cannot equal that of the biological parent. They may start asking questions like: "Do you think she's a good parent?" Or, "How does he get along with the kids?" These questions are hard to answer. If the custodial parent says the new mate is a good stepparent, the grandparents may not believe it. Certainly, the custodial parent will not answer with, "No, he's not a good parent; actually he's horrible," or "Oh, yes, she loves to mistreat them."

First meetings of the entire family can almost have a "looking glass" effect. The grandparents watch the stepparent intently to see if he or she is a good parent. This phenomenon is somewhat unique to the stepfamily, but, through honest communication and sharing of feelings, approval is usually given.

One of the most important factors that contributes to the slow acceptance of the stepfamily by the grandparents is the sudden blending of the family. Grandparents are frequently given little time to warm to the idea of this new "family." The first time

Chapter 5   The Role of Children in the Remarriage

around, there was probably a period of dating, followed by the marriage and a honeymoon. A few years might have passed in which the young couple talked about having children. When the wife became pregnant, much fuss was made about choosing names, buying cribs, and decorating the coming baby's room. Friends and relatives may have played a significant role. With the stepfamily, however, none of this occurs. The family is ready-made.

The confusion is doubled when the new spouse brings his or her own children to the marriage. Grandparents are now faced with the problem of coping with new "grandchildren," who they do not even know. All the rules that grandparents had learned about families are of little use when measured against the stepfamily. It is a difficult time for all involved.

Taking Positive Steps

When previously married people with children decide to remarry, they have not only their relationship to worry about, but they must also worry about the adjustments of the children if their new family is to be stable. Following are some positive steps a couple can take:

1. They must keep their relationship as the focus of the family. Problems should be discussed and resolved. The husband and wife should not argue in front of the children, if possible, because public arguing gives the children a chance to believe that the marriage is weak and will fail. Moreover, it allows the children to choose sides, usually with the custodial parent. This will only add to the conflict and anger.

2. A couple should strive for compromise. They should not go in different directions. Disagreements should be settled, because problems that persist fester and grow worse. Seek counseling if issues continue to "fester." Once a solution is reached, partners should stick with it.

3. A couple should forget most of the advice that others offer, and instead do what they feel is right for their family.

4. Partners should avoid bickering with ex-spouses. People who could not agree when they were married rarely agree after they are divorced. The ex-spouse should be kept out of the new marriage.

5. Both parents should provide a nurturing environment for the children. Keeping the lines of communication open, even when it seems that the children do not want to listen, is vital. Parents must offer a united front and not side with the children against each other.

The members of a stepfamily need love, reinforcement, and plenty of positive strokes to each other if the family is to succeed. Since children are usually too young to offer much support, building the foundation of the stepfamily falls to the husband and wife. The strength their relationship provides for that foundation in large part will determine the strength and stability of the family.

Chapter 6
The Influence of the Ex-Spouse on Remarriage

Once they decide to remarry, most people feel that their problems will decrease. Instead, problems may escalate. For many couples this is hard to understand. After all, getting married should be a time of joy, a new beginning, but for couples starting a stepfamily that new beginning is frequently marred by problems from the past.

A major source of those problems is often the ex-spouse. No matter what condition the relationship was in after the divorce—good, tolerable, or terrible—it is likely that the ex-spouse will react negatively to the idea of his or her former mate remarrying. There are many reasons for this dilemma.

Most commonly, the ex-spouse is jealous. He or she does not want his or her ex to love someone else, and may be afraid that this new person will be a better mate. The ex-spouse may be angry because the current relationship with his or her family will be changing. He or she may be confused and fearful that the new husband or wife will take away some of the love of the children. The ex-spouse may feel that the stepparent will be a better parent, and may be upset with the children because they like the new parent. Finally, the ex-spouse may feel lonely because the bonds of the former marriage will now be entirely broken.

Changing the relationship between ex-spouses is hard, but it is necessary if a couple who are to marry want to be successful in their remarriage. Any arrangement should be mutually beneficial and healthy to each person involved, even though the arrangement may not be liked by everyone. Medicine seldom tastes good, but it is clearly necessary to rid the body of illness.

When the issue is remarrying, problems with the ex-spouse usually start at the beginning. Some of the problems are brought on by the man or woman who is planning to remarry. It may seem like one is asking for trouble, but some people actually ask the ex-spouse for approval to get remarried. When a man or woman bases such an important personal decision on the feelings of an ex-spouse, turmoil is already brewing. Each person should make his or her own decision about remarrying. While checking the feelings of the children is important, since they will be affected by the new person to join the family, even here the decision must be made by the adult. Certainly it would be nice if everyone gave his or her blessing to the remarriage, but this is generally not the case. The adults must make the choices they feel are the right ones, because this is the only way they will have the stamina to endure the hard times ahead.

Let us assume that a man does not like his former wife remarrying. He tells her quite plainly that she should be ashamed of herself for bringing another man into the family, a man who has no right to raise their children. What can this woman say? What can she do?

Such a confrontation demands clear communication in which feelings are shared without rancor. She might say something like this: "I'll listen to your opinion, but you must also listen to mine. I have my own life, and I have a right to live it the way I choose. You'll just have to understand that."

Of course, those words sound easy but are in fact hard to say. It is difficult for people to stand up for themselves, especially during times emotions are running high. It is much easier to back down, and tell ourselves that we will handle the problem tomorrow. Unfortunately, tomorrow will not come. It has been our experience that when ex-spouses do not confront the issue of remarriage from the beginning, the problems associated with it worsen.

Chapter 6   The Influence of the Ex-Spouse

June, an administrative assistant for an oil company, felt elated and awful about getting married. "Ron (her former husband) doesn't approve of the marriage and he has the kids siding with him," she said. "The thing that makes me so angry is that Ron never approved of anything I did anyway. He is so damn controlling. That's why I left him. I had a boss at work and I didn't need one at home. But I still seek his approval. And now the kids act just like him. He says it will ruin the children. I'm amazed that he's so interested in the kids now. When we were married, he worked half the time and watched television the other half. I had to beg him to do things together as a family. Now I have a man that really loves me and I think he'll be a good father. I guess they'll all have to learn to live with it."

June's experience illustrates that going on with one's life and breaking old and painful ties does not free a person from misery and hard decisions.

Change is hard and usually receives little support. In fact, most of the people who are affected by the change will resist it. This is particularly true of the ex-spouse.

Manipulation and Control

Many of the problems that arise between ex-spouses have their roots in manipulation and control. One (or both) of the partners wants to control his or her ex, usually because this boosts the ego. Control is exercised through manipulation.

The manipulation by the ex-spouse may be overt or subtle. One of the most common types of overt manipulation is to withhold child support. "Do what I say, or you can forget the check," is the bottom line. Another is to threaten taking the children away in a custody suit. "Do what I say, or I'll call my lawyer and the kids will be mine." Most threats like these, however, are empty. Consulting with an attorney can allay fears that arise from the threats of an ex-spouse. Legalities often become a battleground for the stepfamily, and it is helpful for people to fully understand the terms of their divorce agreements.

Manipulation by the ex-spouse may be more subtle, especially concerning the children. Sometimes the ex-spouse will attempt to pull the children to his or her side. Remarks like, "Isn't it awful that Mom's getting married and spoiling our family?" and, "I don't think Daddy should remarry, because it'll make life miserable for you kids," can stir things up dramatically and lead to bitter arguments. The remarrying couple must learn that they cannot control what their ex-spouses do. Rather they should minimize the damage through frank discussions.

When a problem with an ex-spouse arises, he or she should be dealt with directly. Children should not be used as messengers because their involvement only complicates the problem. Yet, many ex-spouses use their children to communicate because they have trouble talking to each other.

> George, a car salesman, is an example. "I don't know how all this started. I admit that I was resentful of Lisa getting married. And so I started belittling her and Dick. Pretty soon the children got into the act. Everyone was carrying tales back and forth and it really got out of hand. So much damage has been done that Lisa and I barely talk to each other." Such cases are most unfortunate, because once communication breaks down problem-solving becomes even more difficult.

Many issues between ex-spouses arise out of the need to control each other. Because they want to control—which is a reason many marriages fail—they refuse to let go. Even though they are divorced, one or both of the spouses continues to meddle in the affairs of the other.

Just like they ruined the previous marriage, these "control" relationships can reach into the remarriage and cause problems there, too.

> Consider Sue, the helpless ex-spouse. She calls her former husband constantly about countless petty problems: "The plumbing doesn't work," "My car won't start," and, "I can't discipline Johnny... he needs to talk to you." Most males feed on this ego-stroking, but get angry at the same time because of the demands it imposes on them. For Sue's ex who has remarried, it is like having two marriages at once. Undoubtedly his new partner will come to resent Sue's intrusions, and the new marriage will be strained unless Sue's calls are stopped.

Mike is an example of the nonchalant ex. He never makes his child support payments on time, and puts off every request that his former wife makes of him. However, he is quick to demand his parental rights and comment on his former wife's lifestyle, as well as what his child needs in a home life. He even makes announcements like, "I will see my son today," regardless of what his ex-wife might have planned. His actions clearly are an attempt at control. If his wife continues to listen to him, she might as well be married to him.

Couples like Mike and his wife are stuck in what we call the biological trap. Because Mike is the biological father, he feels that he can do whatever he wishes in regard to his son. He can forget child support payments, but still take his boy out for ice cream. While showing his son the good times, he is never around when his boy needs the help and encouragement of a father. Caught up in his game of control is his wife.

Still another example is Joe, the sad ex. His life is "over" since his wife left and took the children. Joe is a manipulator, though, who has his ex-wife drive the children several hours to visit him because he is heartbroken without them. Of course, for a variety of excuses, he cannot make that trip himself. As bad as the drive to Joe's home may be for his poor wife, the return of the children is worse, because they feel so sorry for their poor father who simply cannot rebuild his life without them that they are in virtual mourning. The guilt in such families can be overwhelming.

In each of these cases, ex-spouses refused to let go. By doing so, they jeopardized the new relationships of their former mates. They stood in the way of happiness. Every divorced man and woman can choose to live his or her life fully or drown in misery. No matter what the ex-spouse says or does, individuals must make their own choices of how to live.

Some experts advise that divorced persons keep in touch with their ex-spouses, especially when children are involved. They suggest parenting together, talking together, and planning for the children's futures together. We disagree. We have found that very few people are interested in having a friendship with their ex-spouses. Our research shows that most divorced couples "parallel parent" rather than "co-parent." This is where each ex-spouse parents the child according to his or her own methods rather than conferring with each other.

Karen learned this the hard way. "Everything I read said to keep a relationship with Larry. But the truth is, I couldn't talk to him anymore. First, because he ran off with another woman and second, we had nothing in common. Our conversations were so superficial and boring that I just avoided them. The more I saw him, the better I felt about not being married to him. Being a friend meant that I had to be close to him, and I just didn't think it was worth my time."

Sometimes ex-spouses hang on to each other through the children. Long discussions about the children or attending events as a couple with the children do the parents or the children little good. If the children believe that their parents are still interested in each other, they may also believe that their mother and father will reconcile. Thinking that, why should they become involved with the new family? This could undermine the development of the stepfamily. Ex-spouses can avoid giving children false impressions about their feelings toward each other by keeping conversations about the children short and to the point, and by limiting the amount of time they (the adults) see each other. Rather than stepping inside the ex-mate's home, waiting outside for the children to go in might be a better idea.

We have found that most divorced people would like to remain acquainted with their ex-spouses, but without close or emotional ties. Remaining close to an ex-spouse makes it difficult to concentrate on building a new relationship, and puts a new marriage under severe strain.

For most people divorce hurts. Throughout the process a man and woman are angry at each other. Simply because the divorce is finalized does not mean that those feelings disappear. The hurt and anger linger, and it is quite painful to maintain the relationship. Most people want to forget the other person as fast as possible. They want to move on, start a new life. Every time they see the ex-spouse, the hurt feelings well up again.

Making the Stepfamily Work in Spite of the Ex-Spouse

For a remarriage to be successful, and the stepfamily it creates to be strong, we believe that the husband and wife must forget the ex-spouses and focus on the new family. The two factors are often intertwined.

Whenever an ex-spouse takes time from one of the new partners that could be spent with the new family, the new family will suffer. The new mate will likely resent this as well. No one likes to hear about old spouses, and when an ex-spouse keeps intruding on the new marriage, anger, frustration, and conflict can result.

Here is an example, taken from the stepfather's viewpoint. Assuming this man likes the children (which is usually the case), he is trying to develop a relationship with them. This proves to be hard. When his wife talks about her former husband, the children's biological father, the situation becomes more difficult. When Mom brings up a time during the previous marriage when the family went to a special event together, the children quickly share their own stories. This might be a chance for them to feel sorry for themselves, or it may be an excuse to avoid getting close to their stepfather. What Mom does not realize in this case is that by bringing up her ex-spouse, she is undermining the growing closeness of her new family.

The issue of child support makes such situations even touchier. Seldom do support payments cover everything the children need. In most stepfamilies, the stepparent contributes money, time, and emotion to the upbringing of the children. Yet, acceptance of him or her by the children can take quite some time. Thus the stepparent finds himself or herself in the unenviable spot of assuming the burdens of parenthood with few of its rewards.

Now let us look at the mother's position. She must set the pace for family unity. To make the new family work, she must pull out of the old family system. She must avoid getting involved in what the children do with the ex-husband, limit discussion about him, put a stop to the wonderful reminiscing, and stand up for her new husband, the children's stepfather, when necessary. While some of the old experiences can and should be talked about, the mother must make sure the children know that they now have two lives: one with their biological father, and one with their stepfather. This is how it will be. Life moves on and the new family is important.

This is not so easy to do. Often it is easier to live in the past and keep from committing fully to the present relationship. It is easier to drift than row against the current. Sometimes, because they have not entirely broken free from their ex-spouses, people use the image of the ex-spouses as angels that the new partners must live up to. Children resist establishing a relationship with a stepparent because they feel that they are betraying their biological parent. But for a stepfamily to evolve, family members must grow individually and as a unit.

Child Support

Child support payments, for many families, become a serious problem. The purpose of child support is to insure the welfare of the children after their parents divorce. Over 25 percent of ex-spouses, out of anger, irresponsibility, or lack of money, fail to pay. A majority do not meet their custodial payments on a regular basis.

Our feeling on this is fairly clear. If an ex-spouse does not contribute to the upbringing of the children, he or she should not see them. The custodial parent should go to court if necessary to protect the children. Nonpayment of child support not only harms the children, it also puts an added burden on the supporting stepparent, which can lead to resentment that manifests in family strife.

When an ex-spouse refuses to pay, or is unable to pay, an alternative may be adoption of the children by the stepparent. Many children who are adopted in the United States are in fact members of stepfamilies. This is usually more than a matter of coincidence; often it is a matter of family survival, stability and choice.

Some men who remarry find themselves in the unhappy position of paying for two families. While living in one stepfamily, the poor fellow is paying child support for the other. For most men like this, the situation is truly a nightmare. The current wife complains that he gives too much money away, and spends more than enough time with his "other" children, while his ex says that he spends too little time with "their" children and does not give her enough money. Both are probably right.

If this situation is to succeed, the man must set priorities and make them known to his present family. No matter how hard he tries, he cannot spend all the time he wishes with them. Financially, the burden is harder. All the children need his support, but not both wives.

An ex-spouse should attempt to do the best for his or her children with child support, but must realize that his or her former mate will use the money as the former mate wishes. The ex-spouse should never promise what he cannot provide.

A Family Effort

The influence of the ex-spouse on the new family should be minimized. The past should be put behind and the formation of the stepfamily should be looked upon as a beginning. The new husband and wife can set the tone for their stepfamily by insisting on its importance to their children. The new family should be the focus of all family members.

Everyone must make an effort if the family is to succeed, and the adults are the persons who set this example.

Peggy understood this and encouraged her family members from the beginning.

"I knew that the kids would have a tough time accepting me," she said. "Their mother hated me and told them so. Of course, Kenny's two girls weren't thrilled either about their father marrying another woman. But I demanded that I be treated cordially from the beginning and Kenny stood up for me. If the kids were rude, he told them to straighten out. I always treated them with respect too, and I never put down their mother. We also managed to keep the other parents from affecting our family. Eventually the girls grew to like me and actually began confiding in me more than they did their real mother. I guess you could say we worked it out."

Perhaps that last line is most important. While most stepfamilies share common problems, the way they react to those problems is based on the unique experiences and personalities of the family members. Every stepfamily must work out its problems by the family members offering each other caring, sensitivity and support. Building a strong, healthy stepfamily in which the needs of the family members are satisfied and their aspirations encouraged is one of the most difficult tasks the husband and wife of a remarriage face. Yet, the happiness of family members and strength of the remarriage depends to a great extent on the successful development of their new family.

Chapter 7
Integrating the Family

The first few months of a remarriage and stepfamily are hard. It takes perseverance, strength, love, honesty, consideration, and positive control for the marriage to be successful. Perhaps the last factor—positive control—is the most important.

Almost every positive human interaction involves "control." When people are in control of their lives, they feel free, they can grow, and they can achieve success and happiness for their families.

One problem that we see repeatedly with disturbed or unhealthy families is the children being in control, not the parents. To rectify this we teach parents how to "manage" a family. If someone is going to steer a ship, we hope it is an adult rather than a ten-year-old. While parents need not feel that it is necessary to rule their family with an iron fist, they must realize that they are the directors who lead the family in a positive manner. That is what this chapter is about—helping the family to grow, to be successful and healthy.

A major obstacle to a stepfamily's integration is the adjustment of the children. Identity struggles, past family patterns, power contentions, as well as the normal stresses of growing up, can disrupt the family and result in tension and turbulence. Children may deliberately or unconsciously use the turmoil to get what they want. Children can be marvelous manipulators.

Billy is a good example. When his mother remarried, Billy found that he was not receiving the same amount of attention that he was used to. But he quickly discovered that he could get plenty of attention by misbehaving. He could get his mother extremely upset by annoying her at dinner by not eating, throwing a tantrum, or refusing to do his chore of feeding the animals at supper time. Billy, of course, was manipulating his mother for the satisfaction of his own needs and was not considering the needs of anyone else. Inadvertently, by paying him more attention, his mother was reinforcing his behavior.

When his mother contacted us, we decided to call a family conference. After discussing why Billy was behaving as he was, it became easier for his parents to understand what was happening. We discussed a plan of action, talked about everyone participating, and insisted that the parents present a united front. First, we decided that if Billy could not manage to complete his chore of feeding the animals, he could not eat a meal either. Second, if Billy misbehaved at dinner, he missed the meal. That also meant no snacks in between meals (for which he pleaded). He would have to wait for the next meal.

This was the hardest part of the plan for Billy's parents. They felt guilty, like they were starving their child. However, they soon learned that Billy, like most children, would conform to their rules once he saw that his parents were not going to give in to his demands or behavior. It was not long before Billy began eating on time with the rest of the family.

Finally, we talked about positive ways his parents could show Billy attention, and how they could encourage him to do better rather than discourage him to misbehave. Everyone likes to be noticed, and so we worked with Billy's parents in learning how to recognize good and useful behavior. Billy enjoyed the positive, and soon realized that healthy behavior was rewarded.

Chapter 7　　　　　　　　　　　　　　Integrating the Family

Establishing a Family Identity

When we work with stepfamilies, we find that many have trouble establishing a family identity. A family identity is the cement that holds the family together; it is the sense of belonging that family members share, the feeling of "we-ness." It is crucial for the growth of a family.

Creating this identity, however, can be difficult and entails much work. It also requires investment on the parts of the adults and, eventually, the children. A typical stepfamily in America involves a female single parent with children who marries a noncustodial male with children. Often the male will visit his children or his children visit him, but in that case his children are only part-time family members. Sometimes, these part-time children have a minimal role in their father's new family. Sometimes, they can have a greater role. Sometimes, they fit in with their father's new family, and sometimes they can be disruptive.

Parenting in the United States is in a state of confusion and uproar. Even in the nuclear family, parents are having a tough time and are not sure exactly what to do with their children. This state of upheaval in our culture creates an even more difficult situation for the stepfamily, and requires parents to stick together and work from one base of discipline. Too often a new husband and wife forget that parenting involves values, traditions, and personal experiences. The past is not easy to forget, especially for children.

Lisa and Hank argue constantly over their children. "Hank says I'm too easy on them," Lisa explained. "I just feel like they have been through a difficult time and I don't want to cause any more trouble for them. They get to see their real father only once a month. I feel bad I've hurt them so much."

Hank disagrees with that philosophy. "I know the kids have been through a tough time, but that's how the world is. We've got to be doing things around here and all everybody does is think about the past. I'm getting tired of it."

Hank and Lisa each have good points, but their disagreements are not helping the children. Their children, in typical fashion of such situations, have become depressed, act out, and frequently harass their parents.

Like most remarried couples, Hank and Lisa have missed out on the time that first-marrieds have to build their relationship. This time of growing as a couple allows the partners to establish communication and share discussions of how they will manage the future. They have time to talk about children, how they will rear and discipline them. Even with this extra time for preparation, first-marrieds still find parenting to be a most hazardous undertaking.

The stepfamily has no such luxury. Thrust into a marriage with the emotional baggage of a failed first marriage, the husband and wife are desperate to make this one work. The last thing many of them need is to worry about children. Along with struggling to find their identity as a couple, they must also come to terms with being parents and having an instant family. Sometimes the struggle becomes overwhelming.

Mary, an insurance executive, tired of the constant frustrations. "My kids would never accept Tom, and I found myself calling up my ex-husband, Ken, for help with them. When I talked to a therapist about my problems, I mentioned that Tom seemed to be avoiding everyone. It suddenly dawned on me that I was creating the distance. I was used to calling all the shots and when I couldn't, I'd ask Ken, who usually didn't help much anyway. I guess it just felt good to talk to him. I realized that I was keeping Tom out of the relationship. It made sense for me to begin my new family rather than to live in the past. If the kids wanted to do that, then it would be their problem."

Mary's understanding that the new family had to come first, that it had to be the foundation of the relationships of the family members, was a major step. Only by making the new family paramount can the members help their family survive as a successful unit.

Family Members and Their Feelings about the Stepfamily

The different members of a stepfamily will usually view it from their own perspectives. Feelings will vary considerably. We will look at the more typical examples.

The man who marries a woman with children invariably grapples with numerous emotions. He knows that he loves his wife and yet may have very mixed feelings about the new children. Torn in conflict, he expects his wife to always support him, particularly during troubling circumstances with the children. Unfortunately, it is the rare wife who always does. This angers the man, and puts a gap, a separation, between him and his wife, and him and his children. It may also cause anger between the wife and the children. He likes the children, wants to grow closer to them, but there will be times that he resents them. As a stepfather, he does all the things a father does, but without the rewards. He attempts discipline, but may be sabotaged from all sides. Aggravating the problem, he may not only be supporting this family financially but also his children from a previous marriage. This fellow may end up penniless and yet no one thinks he is a good man.

Tom offered his views. "Susan and I disagree on how to discipline the children. I think she's too soft, and so I speak up when I think the kids misbehave. When this happens, she sticks up for them and not for what I say. So, we end up having a big fight and the kids do whatever they want. She keeps telling me she'll support me next time, but it never happens. She gets angry, though, when my kids come over for the weekend and screw up. Then it's my fault because I don't discipline them enough. It's getting to the point where I'm just tired of it."

In this case, Tom and Susan are clearly pitted against each other and the family is becoming the loser. It is crucial that the husband and wife of a remarriage agree on childrearing and discipline, and present the children with rules that are fair and consistent.

Just like the adults, children come to the stepfamily with their own feelings. Believing that their biological parent has betrayed them by bringing a new parent into their lives, the children may resent the stepparent from the start. Judged guilty before the trial has even been set, the stepparent faces high odds. The children may feel jealous, and may try to alter the new marriage. They may feel frustrated and simply try to annoy the stepparent. Even when they like the stepparent, it is not easy. They may pretend that they hate the new parent rather than face feelings they would rather hide.

The mother in the stepfamily is perhaps the most confused by her feelings. If she supports her ex-spouse, the children grow closer to her, but her new husband drifts farther away. If she moves toward her new spouse, however, her children become angry. She is pulled constantly from all sides. Wanting help with parenting, she may reject her new spouse's efforts because they represent changes, for which she may not be ready. Yet in this case, the children usually gain too much freedom and experience problems with adjustment.

> *Linda thought the transition to a stepfamily would be easy. When she and Sam were dating, her children liked him. Even her ex-spouse said that the relationship was good for her. It was after she and Sam married that their life together became confusing.*
>
> *"I think it's a disloyalty problem," Linda said. "The kids feel if they get close to Sam, then Lou will get upset. And Lou has helped reinforce some of that garbage. I think they can love Sam if they give him a chance, and still love Lou. I believe that each person can be important to them if they would give it a chance. Instead, everyone keeps on blaming me for their problems. Sometimes I think they're all spoiled kids and I have to be the parent to everybody. That's probably a problem I have... wanting to be in charge all the time and telling people what to do. Maybe they should just fight it out."*

These examples are quite typical of stepfamilies. Many remarried husbands and wives are confused over what to do, advice from relatives and friends is generally useless, and the couple often end up feeling frustrated and defeated. Chaos results from a clear lack of control and direction.

The Importance of Structure

We believe that for the stepfamily to be successful, structure is essential, particularly during the first few years. The parents must take charge by setting limits and guidelines of how the family will function. These rules can be discussed with family members, but the parents must make the final decisions and hold strong convictions if the family is to succeed.

In families where children are involved, the prospective husband and wife must discuss parenting before marriage. These discussions should not be on vague philosophies of childrearing, but on the specifics. The new couple must come to an agreement on the seemingly minor routines that are in fact integral to the smooth-functioning of the family. Questions concerning eating as a family, what time the children go to bed, manners of speaking to adults and children, TV watching, family activities, how money is spent, and who is responsible for what chores are just some of the issues that can become major points of contention.

We believe that children should take an active part in the household chores as soon as possible. Certainly children as young as five or six can assume some duties around the house. Chores should be non-sexist, which means that five-year-old boys can help wash dishes and seven-year- old girls can help wash the car. The purpose here is not to frustrate children, but to show them that life contains both work and play. We have seen too many adults "protect" their children from being responsible in the attempt of being a "good parent." This happens quite often with divorced parents, who feel guilty over what has happened and want to shield their children from what they perceive as being the harshness of life.

Setting rules therefore is essential, yet many parents find it difficult to come to decisions. To us, no decision is a decision not to act. Couples who do not establish rules of behavior and responsibility risk the deterioration of their family. In the extreme, families without rules or with inconsistent ones create maladjusted family members. Adults owe their family proper consideration.

Once the husband and wife have decided on family rules, they should discuss them with the children. The couple should present them together and offer a unified front.

After the rules are stated, the couple should listen for feedback from the children. Sometimes, the rules may need changing, but they should not be adjusted immediately. Children can be self-centered, wanting to avoid responsibility, and can be quite persuasive or argumentative in their demands. The couple should listen carefully to what the children say, then discuss making changes afterward. The rules that are finally set should be based on what the husband and wife truly feel is right.

Even if there is resistance on the parts of the children, parents should insist that the rules go into effect immediately. Putting rules off only makes it that much harder to institute them later. If there is denial or disobedience, then there must be appropriate consequences.

While we do not advocate physical punishment such as hitting a child (although two-year-olds may require gentle correction), consequences should be meaningful and consistent. We favor those that are logical. For example, if a child does not pick up his or her clothes, the clothes do not get washed. If the child does not show up on time for dinner, he or she does not eat. If the child refuses to wash the dishes, he or she eats from dirty dishes. Deliberate disobedience may result in a restriction of privileges, however we will discuss this in more detail in a later chapter.

While rules are important, the family also benefits from the philosophy that families help each other. This should be a goal of both parents. Children should be taught to appreciate giving to one another. If the family is to succeed, all members must share in the good and bad. This means everyone has chores and everyone enjoys the rewards.

In families where both parents work, the children may have to help even more. The added responsibility they will assume will help them as they grow, particularly when they marry. Children usually adjust to responsibility fairly well, especially when parents provide firm guidance.

Ophelia felt guilty about spending so much time away from the children. "I know we can't make it without my income, but I still don't feel good about it," she explained. "The kids are spending so much time in day care and I really miss them. But that's the way it is, and so the time I do spend with them is precious. I'm finding that I value my time with them more than

Chapter 7 — Integrating the Family

I used to and that I try to make the most out of each moment. Maybe I worry too much. After all, the kids seem to be getting along well."

Ophelia illustrates the point that everyone must be committed to the unity of the family and be willing to sacrifice if the stepfamily is to work. In her case this means holding down a job and making sure that she still provides the proper nurturing for her children. When a couple remarries, everything is shared. The mine-and-yours syndrome leads to divorce. Both husband and wife must give if they expect to receive the benefits of a satisfying family life.

Beyond commitment, there are words that signify togetherness. We strongly suggest that the stepmother or stepfather be called Mom or Dad. Calling people by their title shows commitment both by the parent and child. Calling the stepparent by his or her first name, however, bestows the status of the mail person or gas station attendant. When adults accept the role of parent, they deserve the title. Children have enough love to give to three or four parents. Although they might be angry or refuse at first, children will accept the title if the adults do. In many cases the ex-spouse is more upset with the stepparent being called Mom or Dad than the children are. Unquestionably, change is difficult for everyone in the new family.

As the children call the stepparent Mom or Dad, they establish what we call a "cognitive framework." The more they say the word, the more comfortable they will be with it.

Just as children should call their stepparents by title, stepparents should refer to their children as my son or daughter. This may be hard for some, especially if the children resist, but such acceptance helps to build family unity. Of course, if the children are older, or will be leaving home in a short time, the titles may not be worth the aggravation they may cause. However, with most children titles demonstrate commitment and caring on the parts of both the adult and the child. Acceptance is a two-way street.

Usually the adults have the most trouble with titles. Adults have come to place great significance on names and yet do not realize the use of names within the family. The value of the title Mom or Dad cannot be understated.

Bob agrees with this. "I felt uncomfortable at first when the kids called me Dad, but I have to admit that I liked it. It was really Carol's idea and she supported it even over the kids' objections. It was funny, but after the awkwardness was over and we had sat down and discussed it, everyone felt better. In fact, I started to feel more like a dad and the kids began treating me better."

The idea of commitment to the new family can be achieved only if the custodial parent supports the new parent. This is vital, even when they disagree. It means sticking up for the new parent (even if he or she is wrong), letting him or her be a parent, forcing, if necessary, the kids and the new parent to spend time together, talking about the new parent positively, avoiding taking sides in arguments, and forgetting about the ex-spouse and how things used to be.

While it is natural for a husband and wife to disagree on occasion, they should discuss differences in private. Arguing in front of the children will only remind the children of the previous divorce, or give them reasons to hope that the new family fails. The stepfamily needs stability and the custodial parent is the footing for the foundation.

That stability is tested when the non-custodial parent has visitation rights, and his or her children come to visit for the weekend or occasionally spend the night. When children come to visit, they should follow the family's rules like the other family members. When new rules are created for the visiting children, the children of the custodial parent will likely feel sharp resentment. After all, why should they obey the rules when the stepparent's children do not?

This is a vital point because the non-custodial parent often feels guilty about his or her relationship with the children and tries to make these visits extraordinary events. Rather, we believe, the non-custodial parent should show his or her children a typical family and spend time with them just like the other children.

There is no easy way to integrate a stepfamily, no simple formula a remarrying couple can follow to insure the success of their new family. The family members will be moving into a new lifestyle for which they have no experience. The people who give their new family the highest commitment are the ones who most often build successful family units.

Chapter 8
Establishing a Stepfamily Lifestyle

Every family needs a healthy lifestyle. By lifestyle, we mean a manner of living in which family members work together and respect each other's individuality. Achieving a healthy family lifestyle is a challenging task.

Much of anyone's lifestyle is established through risk and change. For example, the custodial parent of a stepfamily may realize that the manner in which he or she parented in the past marriage is no longer effective. Perhaps he or she needs to be more positive or more caring to allay the child's fears and help the child become comfortable in the stepfamily. This is exciting, but scary, too.

A child also may find that past behaviors need to be adjusted. A girl may find that the affection she felt towards her biological father, but which she never believed she could show, is now welcomed by her new father. This may be a marvelous realization, but the emotions involved can be frightening.

Step by Step: A Guide to Stepfamily Living

Changing one's attitudes and behaviors demands perseverance. Change is never easy and requires a strong commitment to follow through.

Consider the typical man in a stepfamily. Like most men, he finds it difficult to get in touch with his feelings. He may want to get close to his new family, but he is not sure how and is afraid to try. He may want to show affection to his new children, but at the same time says to himself, "But these aren't really my kids. How can I take care of them when I have trouble caring for my own?" The man denies his natural impulse and makes excuses for his behavior with comments like, "Oh, they'd reject me anyhow, and I don't want to confuse them."

Some men become mired in the stepfather-lust situation. These men cannot love a female without lusting for her physical body. While sexual intercourse is natural and a need for men and women, it is detrimental between a father and daughter, due to both family considerations and cultural mores.

Children need the freedom to grow into their sexuality within the family. This is particularly true of girls. Too many men do not understand this process and their wives do not explain it to them. Instead of seeing the girl as "child sexy," they misinterpret natural maturation as "adult sexy." Some men then react in an adult fashion and take the child beyond her "child sexy" to areas in which she is not mature enough to understand. To avoid reacting like this to the girls in the family, the man must always act in a parental fashion.

Most importantly, the man must accept the child's sexuality and be willing to talk about it openly. Because of their own insecurities, people often avoid asking if children understand terms like "making love," the function of their sex organs, or feelings of attraction to a man. If a parent is uncomfortable about sex, the child will sense that and come to fear sex, too.

The father should be able to hold and kiss his stepdaughter in a caring and affectionate manner. However, this should be different than the way in which he holds and kisses his wife. With the stepdaughter the action should be more childlike. A kiss on the cheek is more appropriate than a kiss on the lips.

When incest occurs, it is frequently a family problem. Indeed, in many cases, the mother is aware of, or suspects, the incest but chooses to ignore or deny the problem. However, the male who crosses this "family boundary" and sexually abuses a child has demonstrated behavior that warrants serious consequences. This damage to the step-family may be irreparable.

When a stepfather moves into a family with a teenage daughter, the parents should expect that the girl may be flirtatious with the stepfather. This is not uncommon, especially if the girl likes the stepfather. When the adults understand what is occurring, they can treat the situation as more amusing than threatening. The man should not feel guilty as long as the marital relationship is maintained as the important priority and the behavior is treated appropriately.

Clearly, demonstrations of affection between the husband and wife are important with teenagers. Eventually, the children will come to respect the relationship and find partners of their own. A frank sharing between spouses about feelings and behaviors between father and daughter can keep a natural occurrence of affection from becoming a problem where the adult crosses over the natural boundaries and hurts the child.

Characteristics of Healthy Stepfamily Lifestyles

The husband and wife of the stepfamily model the family lifestyle for the children. As leaders of the family, they are in a position to show what a good relationship is, and how to get close to another human being. Of course this does not mean that the husband and wife cannot make mistakes. Making mistakes is a part of being human. However, the husband and wife set the tone for the marriage through their behavior. Their actions often become the future actions of their children because the children learn from their parents.

When we look at marriage, we regularly see that good couples share some common characteristics. We are convinced it is these characteristics that give the marriage its strength and vigor. We will examine each one in detail.

Caring

The components of caring are love, friendship, and intimacy. Quite simply, caring means showing a loved one that he or she is special and not taken for granted. It communicates the idea that life would not be the same without that person.

In successful remarriages, the partners know how important their spouses are. They accept each other, but also support each other in individual growth. Sticking up for each other is a habit, not an effort. When the husband and wife argue, they do so in private, not public. Moreover, they share a sense of humor, realizing that life has its lighter moments. Happy couples of successful remarriages make a pact that nobody steps between them.

In Jill's first relationship, things like this never happened. "We would yell at each other constantly, and he always belittled me," she recalled. "His remarks were so cutting. I was just never good enough for him. My marriage with Tim is so much different. It was very important from the beginning that we respect each other. If either of us has a problem, we don't knock each other, but instead we sit down and talk or yell, or do whatever we need to get it out of the way. Tim pushed for not arguing in front of the kids and I wholeheartedly agree."

Listening

Listening is a rare quality. It entails that both partners talk and each person is understood. It does not mean that there is always agreement, but rather that each person has his or her say and that the other knows what is being said.

Listening requires recognizing that when something is troubling one spouse, he or she can talk about it with the mate. Good listeners have a way of drawing people out so that conflicts can be resolved.

Listening demands taking time each day to talk and share ideas and feelings. Each person must be actively involved in the other's world and want to hear about his or her partner's day. People who are involved with each other, and know how to listen, can communicate. Such people do not mumble life away, but feel free to express themselves to their partners.

Setting aside some time each day to talk helps insure that sharing takes place. This does not mean that one spouse must always be ready to talk when the other is. That is impractical for most couples. Instead some time during or right after dinner, or after the children have gone to bed should be reserved so that the husband and wife can talk.

Confrontation

Good relationships have a little flame under the cooking pot. If one partner upsets the other, he or she should be told, gently but firmly. David Augsburger calls this "care-fronting." It is vital that partners avoid storing old hurts like squirrels hide nuts in the winter. Hurts, slights, and disappointments must be discussed so that they do not recur. Everything must be put up front, in the open.

While confrontation permits a husband and wife to share their opinions, it should not be a time of yelling and screaming. Rather it should be a process of frank discussion. The "wanting to get back at the spouse" should be avoided. Problems that are shared in the spirit of honesty and cooperation are usually solved.

Couples need to disagree. In fact, we are wary of couples that never argue. That usually signals a dead relationship. When couples thrash out areas of contention, there does not always have to be a winner, because that means there must be a loser. It is more important that opinions are heard and each person genuinely considers the other's feelings and views. This leads to negotiation and compromise, which are always better than competition.

Happiness

Happy couples enjoy life. They realize that misery comes, but that it also passes. These folks are able to weather hardship and work their way through it. They manage to find a smile during the most difficult events. They enjoy each other's company, and find pleasure in simple things. Each day to such people is special and something to be shared together.

Wayne Dyer, in his classic book *Your Erroneous Zones*, describes happy people as "those who like virtually everything about life—people who are comfortable doing just about anything and who waste no time in complaining or wishing that things were otherwise. They are enthusiastic about life, and they want all that they can get out of it. They like picnics, movies, books, sports, concerts, cities, farms, animals, mountains, and just about everything. They like life. When you're around people like this you'll note an absence of grumbling, moaning, or even passive sighing. If it rains, they like it. If it's hot, they accept it, rather than complain about it. If they are in a traffic jam, or at a party, or all alone, they simply deal with what is there. There is no pretending to enjoy but a sensible acceptance of what is, and an outlandish ability to delight in that reality."

Sexuality

There is excitement and electricity between a husband and wife whose marriage is strong. Their love has grown and deepened from the original infatuation that drew them together. They still hold hands, hug each other, playfully care for each other, and are not afraid to demonstrate affection in front of family members. They find their partners attractive and sexually interesting.

Individuality

No matter how strong a marriage is, each person remains an individual who has a separate life. In successful marriages, the partners grow as individuals, and are not actively trying to control each other. Since the partners are confident in themselves as well as the marriage, jealousy is at a minimum. Statements like, "You have to be in by ten," or "Where were You? Spending another night with your friends?" are rare and seldom used. While major decisions are of course made with the spouse, each person has the chance to pursue his or her own path, knowing that personal growth will contribute to the relationship. Each person develops himself or herself, yet continues to care for the spouse.

Wayne Dyer, in his book *Pulling Your Own Strings,* shared, "We can never entirely understand someone else and each of us remains part stranger even to those who love us. It is the weak who are cruel; gentleness is to be expected only from the strong... you can understand people better if you look at them—no matter how old or impressive they may be—as if they are children. For most of us never mature, we simply grow taller."

Chapter 8 　　　　　　　Establishing a Stepfamily Lifestyle

Sharing

The husband and wife of a successful marriage share life and all of its pleasures. There are no terrible secrets or hidden bank accounts. The husband and wife each contribute to the family and try to understand each other, rather than vie in a power competition. Responsibilities are shared and problems become co-projects to be solved.

In his book *Living, Loving and Learning,* Leo Buscaglio points out the need for sharing. "If we ever needed each other, we need each other now. Divorce rates are growing, relationships are casual and mostly meaningless. The suicide rate is doubling, especially among young people. Intimacy is not simple. It's a great challenge to our maturity. It's our greatest hope."

Commitment

People who share successful marriages do not seek satisfaction of marital needs outside the marriage, for this inevitably causes destruction. Even when things are hard, these people will keep working together. There is no backing out of the relationship. They do not use threats—"I'm going to leave you"—to coerce their partner to do what they want them to do. Neither partner fears that the other will leave.

Commitment also extends to the children. Parents are committed to the children, who often share the same values as the parents. The adults carry a sense of responsibility for the welfare of the children.

Commitment may be the most difficult value for the members of a stepfamily to share. A stepparent may have ambivalent feelings toward his or her stepchildren; the children may be unsure of the new parent. Yet, all are expected to be committed to the new family.

Family members need to be able to depend on each other in order to give and have a feeling of security. Much of this reliance on each other grows out of commitment. When the husband and wife are strongly committed to each other, their relationship becomes a model for the children, and the entire family is strengthened.

Unconditional Love

Many people love with conditions. A favorite phrase of these people is, "I love you if...." The inherent message is that the person will give another his or her love only if that individual acts in a certain way. The messages are many and varied: "I love you if you are good... if you eat your food... if you go to school... if you become a lawyer... if you live near us...." The messages go on and on.

Conditional love is especially potent when it is directed toward children. The messages are often accompanied by sadness or tears, which makes the child feel awful. Because the messages are coming from a parent, children usually believe them.

Taken to extreme, conditional love can play havoc with the self-concepts of children. It can make children psychological wrecks. Consider the mother who says to her teenage daughter, "Go out and have a good time. Don't worry about me staying here alone." If the daughter goes out, she disappoints her mother. If she stays home, she disappoints herself and her friends. She loses either way.

Unlike conditional love which is detrimental, unconditional love is positive and healthy. It means accepting and loving another as he or she is. It means separating behavior from love. Sometimes a person, a child for example, can act in an unacceptable manner. While the behavior may upset the parent, the parent still loves the child. There are no conditions to the love. When children learn to love with conditions, they eventually are hurt.

Families whose love is shared with conditions seldom develop healthy lifestyles. Unconditional love, however, can provide the unbreakable bonds that hold a family together.

Guidance

Every child needs structure and discipline. In reality, it is through discipline that parents teach children what freedom is. Strong, successful families provide the guidance to their children that helps the children grow into confident adults.

Freedom and order are inseparable. Permitting children to have unrestricted freedom creates tyrants. Usually, the parents assume all the responsibility for these children, becoming frustrated and angry until the entire family is drawn into a situation of unceasing bickering and conflict. The child who gets everything he or she wants does not learn the rules for successful living. Well-defined restrictions give children a sense of security. They help children to focus their efforts to achieve worthy goals and thereby enhance feelings of accomplishment and success.

Every child needs structure and must learn to participate in the norms of life. When children are given the proper structure, they generally grow into competent adults who are able to contribute positively to society. Clear and consistent guidelines provide family members with direction, which in turn strengthens the family.

Sacrifice

All members of strong stepfamilies, like traditional families, have learned that they must be willing to sacrifice for the good of the family. Living together as a unit places undeniable demands on people.

Children particularly must realize that they are part of a family and that they have a share in the family's success. They must learn that there will be times when they must sacrifice for the good of others, that they must give a little in order for all to gain.

Frequently parents will have to explain to their children what life's struggles are all about. Sheltering children from reality does not teach them about life; rather it distorts life for them. While children should be treated as equal human beings, they should not be considered to be equal in terms of life experiences. Children should be given responsibilities that are appropriate for their maturity and skills.

The need for developing responsibility cannot be emphasized enough. Parents must show responsibility to their children. They must model responsibility in their actions and behaviors. Children in turn need to learn responsibility from their parents. They must be responsible for themselves as well as for others, particularly in the case of younger brothers and sisters. It is important that siblings learn to care, love, and protect each other. Everyone in the family must work together for the good of all.

Along with responsibility comes cooperation. All family members must cooperate rather than compete. This can be hard. Parents are sometimes guilty of pitting their children against each other. "Why aren't you more like your sister?" is a common complaint. "Why can't you get good grades like your brother?" is heard just as often.

Cooperation, like all the other life skills, is taught and parents are the primary teachers. An effective way to teach cooperation to children is to make the children do tasks together where part of the task must be completed by each person. If it is not completed, all assume the consequences. Children can be taught to appreciate their brothers and sisters, and learn that they can help each other through troubles. All family members need to realize that every member of the family is special.

Establishing an effective lifestyle for a stepfamily takes work, commitment, and cooperation. We believe that in any family the lifestyle and leadership of the husband and wife provide the impetus for positive functioning.

It is important that the marital relationship is the primary focus for the couple and that the children develop from the strength of the relationship. Once the husband and wife establish a lifestyle that teaches sound values for the children, the family begins to be successful and fully functioning.

The marital couple must understand that everyone might not be interested in building a strong family unit. Parents, friends, relatives, ex-spouses, and children may resist the idea, but the husband and wife must be determined to overcome the obstacles. As a positive and caring lifestyle is established, family members will draw closer and the family unit will be strengthened.

Chapter 9
Old Memories and the Stepfamily

Besides having an influence on the children and their commitment to the family unit, the ex-spouse can also have a dramatic impact on the relationship of the marital couple. The presence or the "ghost" and memories of the ex-spouse can cause such a rift between a remarried couple that they may consider divorce before giving their marriage a full try.

The connection between ex-spouses can be difficult to break. This connection may continue well into the new marriage, and may prevent the new marriage partners from becoming entirely "married." The continuing connection between former spouses may be psychological, physical, or religious.

Some individuals strongly deny that an ex-spouse is affecting their marriage.

Tony and Joanne provide a good example. When they came to us for therapy, they were considering divorce. We quickly discovered that Joanne still loved her ex-husband and that Tony in her eyes could never live up to his image. Of course, Joanne could not admit that to herself. Frustrated, Tony was giving up on the marriage and had started to seek companionship outside of the relationship. He and Joanne were fighting constantly, and yet we could see that they cared deeply for each other.

When we talked to Joanne, we found that she was in contact with her ex-husband several times a day, usually concerning the children or the house. She rationalized that this was necessary, "since Tony was never around to help." The children were aware of what was happening, and they helped create a crisis each day so that Joanne had to call their father. Hoping to get their mother and father back together, they helped start arguments between Joanne and Tony over how Tony treated them. They were successful in pulling Joanne to their side, and the family in effect ganged up on Tony and rejected him. After a while, Tony felt completely alienated.

Once they understood what was occurring, Tony and Joanne began the work of rebuilding their relationship. We confronted Joanne that her ex-husband had left her and had since remarried. We pointed out that it was unlikely that he would be coming back to her since he apparently was happy with his new wife. Eventually Joanne came to terms with her resistance to getting close to Tony because she was afraid that she would get hurt again.

Tony had to be drawn into the process of strengthening the marriage, too. We discussed with him the need to become more involved with the children and to spend more time at home. His presence was needed.

While we allowed the children to continue making daily crises, we instructed Tony to make parental decisions with Joanne's support. In a short time, the number of problems with the children decreased, which allowed Tony to form a better relationship with them.

While the children continued to see their biological father whenever possible, Joanne pulled back from her ex, letting the children determine their relationship with their father. With the barriers finally down, this stepfamily started to build closer bonds.

Some of the reasons for conflict in a stepfamily are natural. When an individual has been in a serious relationship before, he or she often has expectations of what is to happen in a new relationship.

Chapter 9   Old Memories and the Stepfamily

Husbands and wives of stepfamilies often expect their new spouses to behave like their old ones. This is clearly understandable since they have grown accustomed to certain habits, routines, and behaviors. It is the pleasant ones, of course, that are remembered.

> "He was always so loving."
>
> "She never forgets to cook dinner."
>
> "He was always willing to help the kids with their homework."

If anything haunts the stepfamily, it is the past. The new husband and wife must come to terms with the past if they are to succeed in their new family. But this is not easy. People can place their ex-spouses on pedestals of adulation, especially if they were left behind in the relationship.

> Jim believed that he would never find anyone like his first wife, who had died several years ago. "I told my new wife that she could never replace Sally or be the mother that she was. Women like her are just very rare, and I have to admit that I'll never find another to take her place. Sometimes you have to settle for second best."

Unfortunately, second best is usually not good enough for most people. In thinking about ex-spouses, feelings are often mixed. Parts of the person can be disliked; parts can be liked. It is not uncommon for the person remembering to wish that the relationship had never happened in the first place. Yet, this type of denial can cause the most grief and sadness because in denying the past one also denies growth and change.

When most people remember, they try to forget the worst and recall the pleasant experiences. This is the mind's way of coping. If we dwell on the negative, life becomes miserable and depressing. This is why children who are abused or women who are married to alcoholics have memories of nice events. Even in traumatic events such as rape, the victim will often block out the circumstances in an effort of coping. The problem with this blocking, however, is that somewhere in the mind, the event keeps itching upward until it confronts the individual or the person physically or psychologically deteriorates due to the inhibited anger.

It is not hard to understand that people may like to remember a happy past when thinking about an ex-spouse. The good is recalled, while the bad is blocked out. The opposite extreme is the person who constantly criticizes the ex and claims that he or she is the cause of all of life's evils. This individual is also having difficulty facing the past, but it is a different type of denial.

Denying circumstances surrounding an ex-spouse can be damaging to all of the people involved. For example, we find that clients have a hard time telling their children that "Mom and Dad" had to get married and that the relationship experienced trouble from the beginning. On the other hand, these same parents are shocked and angry if their sixteen-year-old daughter gets pregnant and wants to elope.

Another serious problem that occurs with ex-spouses is the use of children as "spies." After spending time with one of the parents, the children are barraged with questions. Here are some of the typical ones:

"Did he spend money on you?"

"Who is her boyfriend?"

"What did you do?"

"What did you eat?"

"What did he say?"

"Is he going on vacation and spending our money?"

"Is her boyfriend better-looking than me?"

The questions obviously can go on and on. They put the child in the position of being an informer and supplying information that is of no business to the asking parent. Rather than placing such a burden on their children, parents should follow our simple rule: If a parent has a question for an ex-spouse, he or she should ask the ex.

Chapter 9 Old Memories and the Stepfamily

Reasons for Being Afraid of the Past

While there are many reasons why people may be afraid of facing the past, we have found that some are far more common than others. Probably the most common is that when a person admits his or her ex-spouse's faults, he or she is also uncovering his or her own issues.

When a person looks at what his or her ex did, he or she usually played a part in those actions. For every action, there is a reaction. If the husband was selfish, the wife reacted to that selfishness. Perhaps she was an endless giver, who is now ashamed of how she let her husband constantly take from her. If the wife was not a good lover, perhaps the husband did not love her in the right manner. Maybe he did not adjust his schedule to provide enough time for her. While it may be easier to blame the other person for all of the problems in a marriage, those problems are usually a sign of weakness in the relationship. Both partners are usually at fault.

Another reason for refusing to confront the past is that the past may be less threatening than the present. When one clings to the past, the present does not have to be faced. Current problems can be ignored.

The person who is always talking about how good the former marriage was, how wonderful the ex-spouse was, does not want to cope with what is happening now. The new spouse is always made to feel guilty because he or she does not provide as great a lifestyle, or is not as great a companion, as the partner is used to experiences. This living in the past can make life miserable for everyone involved.

The reality is that even if the previous lifestyle was better (and many times it was not), there was a choice made to marry and start a new family. The new family must forge its own lifestyle. Living in the past prevents commitment to the present and provides an easy alternative to confronting current problems.

Tim and Sally are a good example here. Sally always reminded Tim of how her ex-husband fixed cars. Of course she neglected to mention that he did it to avoid spending time with her. Despite feeling inadequate in the area of mechanics, Tim tried hard, but his efforts were never satisfactory. In retaliation, Tim started picking on Sally for the things she did not do as well as his ex-wife. These early battles were only the beginning of the war.

Without question, living in the past stops change for the future. Many people bring mementos of past relationships to a remarriage. Paintings, pictures, furniture, and other material objects evoke vivid memories. These items have some value, but too often people use them to sadly recall the sorrows they have suffered. It is much better when a remarried couple fill their home with the present, which reflects their commitment to the new marriage. Certainly the past can be reflected upon, its lessons remembered, but it should not be viewed as an unhealed wound. The new marriage is what counts.

Bob and Susan could not sit in their old furniture without being reminded of their pasts. Even the children argued over who owned "what." When Bob and Susan bought new furniture, they threw out old memories with their old chairs.

While many people will agree that the past must be buried if a new relationship is to succeed, settling accounts of the past confronts a person with enormous insecurities. One often finds himself or herself alone, and forced to face what he or she has done. Guilt and sorrow for past acts can be a heavy burden.

Still, facing the past helps us to face ourselves. This is the first step to change. Unless one realizes what went wrong in the past, he or she will make the same mistakes in the present. Likewise, one needs to understand what was right in the past so that these behaviors can be nurtured and built upon. Once a person has discovered his or her faults and strengths, he or she must make a firm decision to change the faults into strengths. This is the action part of change. Unfortunately, many people talk about change but never accomplish it.

Chapter 9   Old Memories and the Stepfamily

Achieving Positive Change

Positive change can have a powerful impact on the success of a relationship. A decision as seemingly simple as "This time I will spend more time with my family," can strengthen a marriage significantly. Positive change on the part of one spouse often leads to positive change on the part of the other partner. Individuals begin to support each other, their bonds become firmer, and the marriage grows.

This action part of change is the hardest for all of us. Most of us like to make excuses of why life is so hard, but few of us resolve to make it different. This attitude can be disastrous to a remarriage. The most successful stepfamilies have partners who admit that they are working hard to be the best that they can be despite the amount of work that requires. Such partners are saying to each other, "Our marriage matters and I want it to be successful. I'll do whatever I must to make it work."

Positive changing in a relationship is hard but worth the effort.

> *Jan agrees with this. "I was bringing into this new family stuff that everyone was giving me. My ex-husband, parents, and friends were not approving of my new marriage. Even after I got married, they were criticizing my lifestyle and my new husband. I was going crazy trying to please everyone. Finally, one day I realized that this was crazy. I knew what I wanted and if the people who were close to me didn't understand, then too bad. The funny thing is that after I told all of them how I felt, they apologized and started accepting me as a person."*

One of the best ways to bring about change in a remarriage is to be open to discussing past marriages and their influence on how they affect the present relationship. It is worthwhile for a husband and wife to talk about the rights and wrongs of their past marriages. Following are some questions that can provide important insights:

"How was your courtship?"

"What attracted you to your ex-spouse?"

"What were your marriage and honeymoon like?"

Educational Media Corporation®

"How were the first years of your marriage?"

"What was it like having children (or not having children)?"

"What effects did the children have on the relationship?"

"What were your social life and friends like?"

"Did parents interfere in your marriage? How?"

"What were the sex roles in the marriage?"

"How were your sex life and sexual relations?"

"What events contributed to your feelings about the marriage?"

"What qualities are still the most likable and unlikable in your ex-spouse?"

"When you think about your ex-spouse, what do you remember?"

"How do you feel your children dealt with the divorce?"

"How do you feel about yourself and your past marriage?"

"What were the biggest mistakes you made in the marriage?"

"What is the most important thing you need now in a marriage?"

"What were the effects of career (spouse's and yours) on the marriage?"

"What is a perfect marriage to you?"

"How do you see yourself changing in the future?"

These questions are vital to ask. Many people feel comfortable talking about everything except their past relationships. It is always difficult to discuss past lovers, joys, and sorrows. Sitting down and arranging a structured situation in which each partner talks about the issues on which the preceding questions focus can be helpful and enlightening. The discussion can take several hours, or can be spread over several days. It is crucial for a couple to relate the information to their present lifestyle.

While many couples find that the answers to such questions can help them to understand each other and strengthen the relationship, sometimes information is shared that can hinder a marriage. Nancy and Stan are an example.

Chapter 9 — Old Memories and the Stepfamily

Nancy blamed Stan, her husband, for the failure of their marriage. In the early days of their marriage Stan seemed to have a promising career in business. They had two children and a life together that many believed was the American dream. Nancy in particular was a go-getter, a teacher who was quite interested in her career. After earning a Master's degree, she was promoted to an administrative position. This came with a price, however.

As her responsibilities increased, she and Stan saw less of each other, but felt more burdened by the demands of the children and the maintenance of a household. It was not long before they began bickering and fighting. Stan came to view Nancy as fighting a battle to defeat all males in order to attain a successful career, while she saw him as egocentric and wanting a woman to cook and pick up after him.

Their divorce was a bitter affair with constant arguments over division of their material possessions. Little consideration was given to the other person. This same, unfortunate situation continued after the divorce in the form of arguments over visitation rights, income tax problems, and countless minor irritations.

Nancy quickly met John, who filled the gap in her life that was left by Stan. Their love affair was rapid and they soon married. At first, their marriage seemed fine. However, as the children settled in and the family began trying to find an identity, Nancy noticed that her new marriage was slipping away. She was experiencing the same problems that she had suffered in her marriage to Stan; the only thing that had changed was the face of her husband.

"Are all men such chauvinists?" she asked. The answer obviously is no. But during her courtship with John, Nancy and he failed to discuss the intimate details of managing a house in which both people work. Nancy assumed that John would understand her lifestyle and adapt himself accordingly. John, however, felt that Nancy would change for him. Soon each was demanding that the other adjust.

They hurled a variety of hurtful statements at each other:

"You don't help out enough."
"I expect a nice meal when I get home."
"I'm used to sex on a Friday night."
"We're eating too late."
"You're a slob, just like...."

By the time Nancy and John came in for therapy, they were about to strangle each other. The anger they had for each other stemmed largely from the past.

In helping them sort out their difficulties, we showed them that it was unfair to carry all this emotional baggage into their new relationship. We helped them bring their secrets out in the open, and they began to analyze why their past marriages had failed. Time and again, we are delighted how supportive of each other a man and wife can be once they reveal their insecurities about themselves and their past relationships.

After several months, Nancy and John understood what they wanted to bring into their relationship by "choice" and not out of habit. They also learned to recognize the needs of their marriage and develop new patterns of behavior that strengthened rather than weakened their relationship. Just as importantly, they tried to share their concerns openly when either of them had a problem.

John and Nancy are not an unusual stepfamily. Indeed, situations resulting from past problems can become explosive if not defused early. A good example is the couple that discusses some matters before marriage, but then changes their ideas soon after the wedding. Perhaps they agree to change the behaviors each believes contributed to the failure of their previous marriages, but they find it is difficult to change.

Joe, for instance, used to nag his ex-wife about dressing nicer and looking sexier for him. After a while, he started nagging his new wife about the same things. Ally, who was insecure and dependent, feelings that led to depression and the need to manipulate her husband, became even more depressed and manipulative with her new husband.

Chapter 9 — Old Memories and the Stepfamily

Breaking out of old patterns can be difficult. Many of these patterns are learned in childhood and are modeled from the same-sex parent. This is why women who have alcoholic fathers marry husbands who are alcoholic or become alcoholics. These women have learned from their mothers how to take care of an alcoholic. For years they have witnessed the tragedy of drunkenness every day. The patterns become so ingrained in them that they do not realize how they are following learned behaviors.

When a person looks at his or her first marriage through honest and critical eyes, he or she will likely see that several factors contributed to its failure. For most couples the most important factor is the relationship. The way a person interacts with his or her spouse, the support (or lack of) given to each other, the amount of encouragement, sharing, and love, all help set the tone for a marriage. Unquestionably, both husband and wife contribute to the success or failure of a marriage. Ignoring the past and its lessons limit one's effectiveness and chances for success in the future.

Examining one's "family of origin" therefore can be quite helpful. Trying to understand the relationship of the parents can provide valuable insights as to how one behaves in his or her relationships. Many people struggle to find balanced sex roles in their marriages. Much of what haunts both males and females sexually are the roles they observed and learned from their parents. Even though American life has changed dramatically during the past few decades, many people find it hard to break out of the type of sex roles they learned as children.

Generally, traditional sex roles are outdated and are proving to be ineffective in our fast-paced society. Economic factors, educational levels, child-rearing patterns, and cultural changes have impacted American life, particularly the American family. Expecting sex roles to stay the same in a society that has advanced technologically and socially in such great strides is ludicrous.

Marital difficulties often emerge from the reality that few of us have experienced the new sex roles before we are forced to assume them. We had no models of these roles when we were children, and must develop them as adults.

Most couples have trouble with these changes. Unfortunately, there are no simple answers. Over the years we have found that the most important ingredient to successful marriages is a willingness to talk, negotiate, and compromise over problems. Breaking with the past and living in the present relationship is essential if a couple is to have a chance at compromise, because only by clearly understanding the past can individuals hope to understand their feelings and needs in the present. Dealing with the demands of the past must be discussed openly by partners so that they can understand how those demands affect current problems, needs, and decisions. Only after understanding can change happen.

For success in the stepfamily, the relationship with the ex-spouse must be put in proper perspective. The term "ex-spouse" means exactly what it says. One is no longer married to his or her ex and is no longer bound by that commitment. If there are children, the custodial parent does what he or she believes is right for them and not necessarily what is best for the ex-spouse.

If there is a cardinal rule to follow regarding ex-spouses, it is this: Never choose the ex-spouse over the present spouse in any circumstance. When the ex-spouse is chosen over the present mate, problems are usually worsened.

Chapter 10
The Role of the Custodial Parent

The role of the custodial parent in the stepfamily is the most crucial and the most difficult. In most divorce cases in the United States in which children are involved, the mother is awarded custody. Even with the changing of society's norms, this is often the rule and anything else is the exception. Moreover, these decisions, based on cultural factors inherent in our society, limit the male's role as a single parent.

In our opinion, women have a decided advantage in seeking custody for three reasons:

1. Women are usually more affectionate to the children and are better able to give the emotional support children need. This is especially true of young children. Many men have trouble dealing with emotional issues and find it hard to show affection to their children. Carl Whittaker, a well-known family therapist, summed it up succinctly when he said, "If I could have three more sets of kids, maybe I could learn to

love." It may be even more difficult for a man to love and care for children that are not his own offspring. Being a stepfather frequently demands more commitment and involvement than being a parent with one's biological child. The stepfather must first establish a relationship with his new children before any bonding can take place.
2. Women are trained in the essentials of daily caring for children. Most women can cook, know how to talk to teachers, and can accomplish many of the household and childrearing chores that make men uncomfortable. As former school counselors, we noticed how many conferences were attended by mothers, but had few fathers. School conferences are just not the father's place—at least from the perspective of many men. Even male comedians joke about their inability to cope with changing sex roles and the changes that are taking place in the family. We heard one comic remark that he learned important things when he was young that have helped him cope with life. These included playing baseball, kicking footballs, and watching Mom. Having a baseball bat doesn't help cook dinner!
3. Women are used to caring for children and are comfortable in this role. Women were often babysitters when they were growing up, and are familiar with the developmental crises that occur with children. Usually it is the women, who as children watch their brothers and sisters, even when they may not be the oldest.

While we are certainly not saying that men cannot learn to do these things well, we do believe that most men must learn how to do them as adults. They are not taught these skills from birth like women are, and this can be a significant disadvantage for the male when he is in the courtroom and a judge is deciding who has the best skills for being the custodial parent.

The advantage that women may enjoy in regard to custody, however, comes with a price. Women who are trained to be "carers" of children may encounter other problems. One of the most significant is that a stepfamily needs a strong and assertive woman for its survival. The woman, who is the custodial parent, will often be torn, her loyalties divided. At the same time she will be experiencing numerous other emotions, including anger, depression, and guilt. Furthermore, she may feel that she must protect her children, while at the same time nurture them with a strong hand. She, and not the male, must be the caretaker and stable unit within the stepfamily. The family will rely on her strength. She may sense that her new family's survival depends on her.

Unfortunately, most women are ill-prepared for this battle, and become very unhappy because of it. The on-the-job training is unlike anything they have ever experienced. It is hard to know what is right when emotions are in turmoil.

A good analogy is the boxer who keeps getting hit with blindside punches. If he turns around and blocks the punches and fights back, he has a chance of winning. If he does not block and fight, he will eventually be beaten. His task is made more difficult because he can never be sure where the next punch is coming from. He finds that he reacts more than initiating action. Yet, if he continues to do that, he cannot win.

The custodial mother finds herself in much the same position. Society and her family keep hitting her from her blind side with unrealistic expectations or "guilt trips" over how terrible life is for everybody. This woman may soon start to feel that the burdens of the world are on her shoulders alone, and that there are no solutions to her family's problems. However, with a sound understanding of her specific circumstances and the motives of those around her, she can gain a clearer perspective from which she can make better decisions for herself and her family.

The Importance of Assertiveness

It is disappointing to us that so many women are not taught to be assertive. Many have trouble with the very idea of being assertive. There are few role models from which women can choose, whether in business or at home, and many back away from offering their opinions and thoughts.

For most women, their mothers were not assertive and were probably more manipulative when trying to attain a goal. Even when a woman determines to be more assertive, her assertiveness is seldom reinforced. Most men do not like it because it threatens them and takes away much of their power in a relationship. Other women do not like it either, because it makes manipulation by them more obvious. When a woman breaks the code and becomes assertive of her rights and needs, she often finds that people become angry with her.

In reality, assertiveness is just another word for clear communication. Assertiveness enables a person to state his or her ideas, needs, and desires. People who can state their minds in a caring but straightforward manner usually expect the same from those with whom they speak. This kind of open conversation can eliminate the games people often play and can be both frightening and healthy. It is healthy because of the honesty, and frightening because the facades are down.

The advantage of effective communication to the stepfamily cannot be understated. When spouses can talk to each other, or to the children, or even to relatives and friends honestly and openly, the air is cleared and everyone understands exactly where everyone else stands. This is one of the most crucial steps in the growth of the stepfamily. It opens the way for family members to forge intimate bonds.

Marsha learned the art of communication the hard way. "When I got divorced, I was really confused," she recalled. "I went to my friends and instead of help all they gave me was hassle. Go back to your husband! You're leaving a good thing! Hell, I didn't need to hear that. All I wanted was somebody to listen to me. My parents weren't much help either. They acted like I was a terrible sinner, and that I could ruin my kids' lives. All of this was too much for me and so I started talking to a therapist.

Chapter 10 — The Role of the Custodial Parent

"After a while, I figured out that they were crazy and not me. Real friends wouldn't talk to me this way. So I finally started to stand up for myself, and, you know, people started to treat me better. I guess they just didn't understand how I felt and what I was going through."

Sometimes, what people think becomes a wall that keeps them apart. This is another reason why effective communication is so important to families.

When we work with stepfamilies, we teach assertive skills in communication to all family members, and particularly to the mother. Because most women have been trained to be the "carer and giver," it is hard for them to demand their rights and not feel guilty. If not managed effectively, this guilt can become a heavy burden.

It is vital that the mother learn to express her feelings to everyone involved, including the children (from all marriages) and spouses (from all marriages). The following story illustrates this well.

Once there was a woman, Karen, who had a friend, Rhonda. Rhonda loved to talk. When she talked, she stood close to Karen, stepped on Karen's foot, and stayed on it all the time she was speaking. Not wanting to offend Rhonda, Karen never told her about her habit of stepping on feet. One day, though, Rhonda was stepping on Karen's foot particularly hard. Finally Karen summoned courage and said: "Get off my foot." Of course Rhonda did, for after all, she did not want to hurt Karen. Finally aware of Karen's feelings, Rhonda did not step on her friend's foot again.

We believe that family members must tell each other when it is time to get off their feet. There is no justification for any family member to hurt another.

While there are many situations in which family members take advantage of the mother, three in particular warrant close examination.

The Ex-Spouse and the Woman

Many women find that the courage they used to sustain themselves through divorce vanishes soon afterward. In the typical divorce, everything is painful: settling the property, dividing finances, determining custody, negotiating child support, and agreeing on visitations are just some of the issues that must be addressed. After all this many women feel emotionally exhausted. Although no longer married to the former husband, the woman still must maintain contact with him, especially in regard to the children and particularly if she is the custodial parent. For too many former partners, this relationship becomes manipulative and volatile. Bitterness soon blocks communication and complicates the simplest problem.

This is what happened to Diane, an accountant with a major oil company. "I can talk to lots of influential people during the day," she told us, "but every time I heard Kevin's voice I cringe. He walked out on me and I still can't forgive him. I know it sounds mean, but I try to get back at him as much as I can. If he wants to see the kids, then he can pay for it. I was so nice to him, and all I got was a divorce in return. It seems like we can't talk about anything without getting into a fight. I'm tired of it."

A major problem for many women is their need to "give." This need can be easily manipulated. Here is a common example.

The woman feels guilty that the non-custodial father does not see the children enough. The father aggravates the situation by moaning how terrible life is for him. When the father is adept at this ploy, he can convince the children to side with him. It does not matter that this was the same father who seldom did anything with his children during the marriage, because when the children are with their father now life is upbeat and fun. The father creates the perfect environment for the typical child's egocentric behavior that believes in "getting all I can get."

Chapter 10   The Role of the Custodial Parent

Debbie offered a clear insight here on a complex situation. "When Glenn would take the kids out for junk food and video games every weekend, I used to get angry," she said. "Here I would be washing their clothes, making dinner, and getting them to school without a word of thanks. He drops in on the weekend and it's like Johnny Carson walked into their lives. It's all smiling faces.

"But then a friend in a similar situation talked to me and I think I understand things better. I forget that he misses out on a lot of things, too. He's not there when the kids share about school, or if they have a big problem, or when they need someone to care. Glenn was not very open with his emotions so I guess if he can't buy them things, there would be nothing left. To be honest, at times I feel sad for him.

"As the kids are getting older they seem to be drawing towards George, their new dad, because he can talk to them. In fact, the kids tell me Glenn keeps putting George down with abrasive comments so I know it must be bothering him that the kids like George."

It is quite common for the non-custodial parent to behave in a manner that infuriates the custodial parent. The actions remind us of the adolescent who is searching for freedom and waiting to retaliate at the same time. Parenting is forgotten by the non-custodial parent, and the custodial parent (most often the mother) ends up being the disciplinarian who places restrictions on the children. In many cases the non-custodial parent will agree with the custodial parent, but then does not give support.

Here is an example.

Joe, the ex-spouse, has no family of his own and maintains contact with his ex-wife's parents so that the children may enjoy a sense of normality. When the children visit the grandparents, Joe visits, which amounts to extra visitation time. The grandparents are placed in an awkward position. Obviously they do not want to ask him to leave, and when Joe just stays they invite him to supper. The children think it is like old times. They even remark how things have not changed that much.

Of course, their mother is furious with this situation, but she cannot control Joe's behavior. Although she tells him her feelings, and he agrees with her, he continues with the same behavior. She is then forced to teach her parents the art of saying, "No," or "We're busy," or "Our daughter said that this is not your visitation time and you agreed." Only when the mother counted the time spent with the grandparents and children as visitation time for the next month did the situation change. She had to be tough for her family.

She was also well within her rights. She had arranged the time so that the children could remain close to their grandparents. She had mentioned to her ex that this would be a good time for the children and grandparents to be alone. When her ex-spouse deliberately used the situation for his own advantage, he alienated his ex-wife and her parents.

We believe that deliberate behavior like this should have consequences, and hence we agreed that using this time as visitation privilege was justified. While it certainly was important to allow the children time alone with their grandparents, it was also important that the children realized the family situation had changed. Their new father was the person who now had a relationship with their grandparents, and not the ex-spouse. The members of stepfamilies must understand that the unity of the new family comes first, and that old family ties are less important.

Another problem occurs when the ex-spouse (the father in this example) denigrates the mother and new stepfather in front of the children. Since this can be quite upsetting to everyone in the stepfamily, it is essential that the mother lends her perspective to the situation. She should tell her children that she had good reasons to divorce their biological father, and that there are two sides to every issue. This should not be done in a spiteful manner, but explanations should be clear and the record should be set straight.

It is also vital that the ex-spouse stay out of the stepfamily's house as much as possible— physically, psychologically, and verbally. Unusual as it may seem, some of our clients have had ex-spouses spend weekends with the children in our clients' houses. Such arrangements seldom work, and usually lead to conflict and resentment.

Discussion about the non-custodial father should be limited in the new family. His place is when the children are with him. While children will be concerned about their non-custodial parent, and these concerns should be discussed, the talks should avoid rattling on about Dad and how great a father he is. This only makes it harder for children to adjust to the new family arrangement and warm up to their stepfather.

The mother must take the lead in solving family problems, and point out to family members that everyone's attention should focus on the current family and not the old one. Members of the stepfamily must live in the present; the past should remain in the graveyard.

The Children and Mom

Children can make life in the stepfamily difficult for the custodial parent (usually the mother) and constantly try to place her in conflicting situations. Because they are unwilling to commit to the new family, the children may choose to vent their anxieties on their mother.

Children who are unhappy with the stepfamily will frequently try to drive a wedge between their mother and stepfather. There is a simple test to find out if this is happening. If a husband and wife fight continually about the children. Even their time alone feels tense—they are having troubles.

> It took Julie a while before she realized that this was happening in her family. "The kids seemed to be always talking about the past and arranging problems so that either they or I had to call my ex-spouse almost daily. After a while, I found that I was neglecting Todd and that the kids were also avoiding him. So I started to pull out and kept spending more time with Todd. Boy, did the kids get angry!
>
> Even my ex-husband tried to get me in the act by saying that he needed to talk to me each day about the kids.
>
> "Well, I stuck to my guns and in a crazy way the kids respected it. I told them they could live in the past all they wanted, but I was in love with Todd and that they were missing a good thing. Finally, they came along and now life is a lot easier."

In many cases the mother must work hard at developing a relationship between the children and their new father. She must support him, and suggest activities for the family to do together, as well as activities that the children can do with their stepfather without her.

If the children say negative things about the new parent, the mother must either ignore them or say positive things. When the children misbehave, or refuse to conform to the new family rules, they must be disciplined. Allowing the children free rein will result in chaos for the entire household. Children will always test their parents.

Chapter 10 The Role of the Custodial Parent

When the new spouse's children come to visit, they should be treated with respect and love, but all of the children must obey the rules of the house. Children must be shown how to get along, and none should be treated with special favor. Sometimes, the father whose children are visiting will want to treat them better—to make up for the hurt of the divorce—but he cannot do that. Messages like "They're special," "They deserve extra privileges," and, "He loves them more than us," can be disastrous truths for the stepfamily. Everyone must be treated the same, and special circumstances must be disregarded.

We always stress that love, caring, and discipline can break down any walls in regard to children, no matter how high they might be. Consistency brings success.

The New Father and the Children

The most difficult situation for the woman is being stuck between her new husband and the children. As we have already stated, the wife owes her primary allegiance to her new husband. However, the husband must also make a commitment to his wife. Sometimes there are major problems with that process.

Some men do not want children. When they marry a woman who already has children, serious problems inevitably result. All family members are likely to be miserable, and in time the father may feel forced to leave the family. A woman should never assume that the man will be able to change his mind about children after the wedding. It seldom happens.

While some men do not dislike children, they may refuse to be parents. Their feeling is that the children belong to the wife, and it is her responsibility to raise them. In fact, however, once the man and woman are married, the children are theirs together. The strength of the stepfamily largely depends on the man becoming involved with the children, as well as with his wife. The commitment of any member to the stepfamily deepens with involvement.

There are also some men who believe that their own children are better than the children of the new wife. Such attitudes only bring anger and hostility. Everyone in the stepfamily must be treated equally with love and respect. This point should be discussed from the beginning and made clear to all family members. The mother and father must share in the raising of the children.

Chapter 10 　　　　　　　　　　The Role of the Custodial Parent

The Male Custodial Parent

While many of the issues confronting male and female custodial parents are the same, the men face some unique problems. Although women usually receive the custody of the children following a divorce, men also may be granted custody. This usually occurs in cases of the death of the former wife, or when the wife is deemed unfit by the legal system because of severe psychological disorders, a history of crime or drug abuse.

It is still rare when the man is awarded custody because he is judged to be the better parent or provide the better environment for the children. Of course, some women do not want custody of their children because they view themselves as poor parents or wish to concentrate on their careers, or they may simply abandon their children as do some men. Whatever the reason men receive custody of the children can have important effects on the stepfamily.

The death of a spouse.

When the biological mother dies, the family may plunge into an extended period of mourning and a new spouse may have trouble living up to the image of the real mother. Competing with the "mythologized" ghost can be impossible as the dead parent takes on the persona of a saint. While some of these families grieve too much, others may not grieve enough, their emotions tied up inside until they become depressed and refuse to move on with life.

The ex-wife is chemically dependent.

These women are particularly damaging to the family when they are actively using. They hurt everyone around them. When they are clean, they may be sweet and promise the world to the children, who then fantasize how great their real mother is. However, when using, these parents are nightmares. They may emotionally, verbally, or physically abuse their children. Chemically-dependent parents are destructive. Even after treatment, we recommend that they have restricted visitation with their children or have restricted visitation until they have been clean for

Educational Media Corporation® 　　　　　　　　　　　　　　　107

two years, and then begin working at building a relationship. When these parents are allowed to interfere with the stepfamily, the members of the new family are constantly trying to repair the damage they cause. The new family is prevented from becoming a unit.

The ex-spouse has a psychological or physical disorder.

Sometimes a handicap, a stroke or cerebral palsy, for example, prohibit a parent from assuming the full responsibility of being a parent. If children are taught properly, they can maintain a strong relationship with the parent that does not preclude a good stepfamily relationship. However, if this parent takes advantage of either the ex-spouse or the children, serious problems can occur.

Psychiatric disorders can be more difficult with which to cope, particularly if the children feel that they are somehow to blame for the parent's condition. This happens even though the children may not be able to think of anything that they did wrong. Some of these parents will tell their children that they are to blame. It is important to protect the children from these parents and to free the children from guilt when they believe they are responsible for the parent's behavior or the parent blames them.

The abandoning parent.

Children often feel confused and hurt when a parent leaves them for no apparent reason. They often think that they are the cause. Custodial parents sometimes make the mistake of trying to shield the children from the idea of abandonment. This is usually a mistake, because the children will fill in the gaps of their knowledge with what they believe to be true. The truth should be discussed calmly and clearly, so that the children understand what happened. Children who are abandoned often feel badly about themselves, and the best way to help them is to give them support based on honesty and love.

The non-involved parent.

Just like men, women can be self-centered, pursue career or love interests, and reject their children. Unlike men, however, women who do these things may cause more damage because such behaviors are less expected of them and the child may not understand why they are doing it. Again, the children may blame themselves or be angry with their parent for the neglect.

Whenever the non-custodial parent is psychologically destructive, chemically dependent, or shows some other behavior that can hurt the children, the custodial parent must closely monitor the relationship between the children and the ex-spouse. If necessary, contact should be limited; if necessary, it should be stopped. With an ill parent, children need to discuss their feelings, and the custodial parent must give them the chance to do so. In the case of abandoning or neglectful parents, the custodial parent should limit contact. The ex-spouse should be made to demonstrate consistent caring behavior before she is permitted to see the children regularly.

Too often custodial parents make decisions because they are easy, or on the belief that children need to maintain contact with their other biological parent. Maintaining contact with an irresponsible, psychologically unhealthy or destructive parent can cause much greater damage to the child than having no relationship at all. Children need to be protected from people who might hurt them. They experience enough trauma from growing up in today's world besides adding deliberate hurt from significant others.

Men face many other problems when they are custodial parents. Caring for a child is something most men are not prepared to do. As the female custodial parent must learn to assume more of the traditional male roles, men must learn to be more nurturing and giving to their children. They must be both father and mother. That male custodial parents tend to remarry within 12 to 18 months after their divorce may be related to their discomfort of having to care for their children. Still, although it is frustrating to them, men can be quite capable in these roles and most find their increased time with their children to be rewarding.

> Joe, an accountant, relates his experience. "Before I married Marie, I was having difficulty making it. The kids were small—1 1/2 and 3—and sometimes I didn't know what to do. We had moved to a new area for my job and my 'ex' just left me and the kids for another guy. She said she was tired of being responsible. I couldn't believe it. With a new job, I wasn't able to go back home and nobody knew what I was facing. The boss at work was demanding and sometimes I'd miss meetings because the kids were sick. He started giving me hints that I wasn't doing my job. Thank God I found Marie. She practically saved my life and really loved the kids like they were her own. Marie is really helping out and she has freed me up a bit to concentrate on my job. But you know, I kind of miss the kids and get a little jealous that she has more time with them."

Beyond balancing everything, the male may expect too much from his wife and stepmother of his children. He may push her to become involved too quickly, and the children may feel forced to instantly love her. As with any stepfamily, everyone needs time to adjust. Members need to discuss what everyone's role will be and the male needs to protect his new wife from assuming too many tasks within the family too soon. Unfortunately, the children may resent any involvement by the new wife as an intrusion. This is particularly true of adolescents. Younger children, on the other hand, may desire her involvement and see her as more "caring" than their father.

Whether the biological mother or father is the custodial parent, or if the biological parents can succeed with joint custody, the most important issue regarding the children is for the parents to provide love and support. The adults of the stepfamily must become the strong role models that children need. Two parents in the house is a more natural and stable situation for children, allowing them the opportunity of observing two or more adults who, although they may look at the world differently, still live productive lives.

Chapter 11
Dilemmas of the Stepparent

Although they are both raising the same children, the stepparent's role and concerns are different from those of the custodial parent. Most often, the full-time stepparent is a man, a role that entails unique considerations. Although female full-time stepparents are increasing, the woman of the typical stepfamily is a stepparent on the weekends or during summer vacations. Still, no matter which sex the stepparent is, the role is a "damned if I do, and damned if I don't" one. The problems often far outweigh the rewards, particularly in the early years of development. However, with courage and perseverance, problems can find solutions.

The Male Stepparent

John is a common example of the male stepparent, and may also be viewed as a trapped father. Having been married for 15 years, his divorce settlement put him in deep financial trouble. While making significant child support payments, he saw his two boys on Wednesday nights and Sundays. Two years after his divorce, he remarried Sally, who had a young son of her own. John grew to love this boy like his own sons. A year later, he and Sally had a daughter.

All these children and families were expensive. After several years, John slipped more than $18,000 into debt, but this was only a part of his problem. He felt that no one cared about him and his life.

His ex-spouse, for example, constantly called him and berated him for being an inadequate father. "I can't do it alone," she would say. She would then demand items that were not a part of their legal agreement, and tell the children that their father was cheap and was ruining their lives.

For John the answer seemed to be to spend more money on his two sons of his first marriage. Unfortunately, whenever he did spend money on them, Sally would complain.

"All your money goes to her and those kids," she would say. "What about us?" John was hard-pressed to find an acceptable answer.

When his sons came to visit, the house would become a disaster. The boys scorned Sally and the other children in an effort to gain revenge for not having the family they wanted. Intolerance strained nerves and resulted in constant tension. The fights became unbearable with everyone involved. Because of the unceasing chaos, John and Sally fought, too.

John searched for a way out of all this, but his problem was a complex one. He could not control his ex-wife, and he needed support from his present wife. Sally, however, was reluctant to give him support because she felt that he was neglecting her and her family. Still, she was the key. She needed to stand beside John while at the same time make her feelings known to him in a calm manner.

In therapy, Sally's leadership and involvement in the family were increased with significant results. She and John were taught how to communicate their feelings and concerns to each other in the spirit of open-mindedness. This cleared the obstacles that blocked the way for behavioral change. Sometimes the dynamics of the stepfamily place people in situations in which they do not want to be and in which they feel uncomfortable. Avoiding these areas, however, only aggravates these situations. When faced in the early-going, problems are usually manageable and can be solved more easily.

The male stepparent is often placed in difficult circumstances. Because of his children with his former wife, and the children he has with his new wife, a man may be emotionally committed to two women. While it is impossible to control his ex-wife, a man can, and must, break away from her. His desire to maintain a relationship with his children can be satisfied while limiting his contact with his ex-wife. He must be willing to make the necessary effort.

Some men find this quite hard to do. We have worked with couples where the male will deny that problems with his ex-wife are even happening. But while he may say there are no problems with his ex, his actions tell a different story. In many cases, he speaks to her on the phone every day, gives her money, shares secrets, and fixes things around the house. Occasionally, he may even have sex with her.

Few marriages can withstand this type of pressure. The behavior borders on the male having an acceptable mistress. While some type of relationship with the ex-spouse is usually necessary over the children, a fine emotional line must be drawn that is acceptable to the new spouse. Our feeling is that the more the ex-spouse is kept out of the stepfamily, the better the stepfamily will function.

While legal agreements that were accepted should be honored, any new or extra benefits should be agreed on by the divorced man and woman, as well as by the new spouses. For the man, the strain of trying to be a good father and providing everyone with everything can be too much. Agreements sometimes have to be adjusted. It is unrealistic to assume that agreements made at the time of the divorce remain unchanged even though the lives of the individuals change.

In our practice, we have found that in most cases, because of the financial strain of supporting two families, someone is going to be deprived of money. We believe that the deprivation—if it must come—should come at the expense of the ex-spouse. The male stepparent's allegiance must be to the new family, while he should honor his financial responsibility to his children.

The Female Stepparent

For the female stepparent, the emotional intensity is just as high even though the conflicts may be different that those of the male. Since women are often better in "caring" than males, the emotional dilemmas of becoming a new mother can be confusing and troubling.

Stepmothers are frequently seen as evil women because they are the ones who set the character and structure of the new family. Moreover, they are usually present in the house more than the man even if both are working. Having to assume this position of emotional responsibility and bonding can be a great burden for the mother of the stepfamily. The children may be reluctant to attach to her because they may believe they are being traitors to their natural mother, or they may sense the emotional commitment the new mother represents and this frightens them. Since stepmothers often set the family rules and guidelines for behavior, they are frequently viewed as "deprivors" rather than "carers." The stepmother thus becomes the enemy in the eyes of the children.

We counsel that stepmothers should proceed slowly in assuming their position in building the unity of the family. She should not jeopardize her beliefs about what the stepfamily should be, but she should move with caution and be attuned to the feelings of the family members. In other words, if she senses that she is moving too fast, she should pull back but without sacrificing principles.

The custodial father must, of course, be supportive of her actions, for the children can be expected to manipulate one parent against the other. Parents must realize that they are often viewed as being "mean" when they say no, and this can be even more true in regard to the stepparent. If the stepparent retreats from principle and gives in to the children to be liked, the respect of the children will never be gained and major problems will follow.

Expanding the Role of Stepparent

Winning the respect and acceptance of the children is not the only battle for the stepparent. Expanding the role, and moving from friend to actual parent with all that the title implies, is a slow but essential process. Family members, particularly the children, are likely to have trouble making the adjustment.

Jack found the role change from friend to parent to be a hard one. "The kids talked to me about everything before Lillie and I got married," he said. "Afterwards, it took a while for them to accept me again. I had to set down rules just like Lillie so that

I wasn't the good guy all the time. But after a few months they grew to understand me and care for me deeper than they had before. I guess it was worth all the aggravation."

There are several steps a couple can take to make the change from friend to stepparent easier for the family. Perhaps the most important is the awareness of the husband and wife that such a change is necessary. Before the marriage, the man and woman should discuss the transition from friend to parent. What effects will this have on the family? How will the children react? What rules should be set down? How should discipline be carried out? Couples should share their feelings honestly on these and similar questions. An agreement on all important issues should be reached. Respect is obviously a key to the entire process of adjustment, and it includes courtesy, involvement, caring, and a reasonable effort on the parts of all family members.

After the marriage, if the process is not progressing as expected, the husband and wife need to share their concerns. They must speak up.

"At first I couldn't believe this was happening to me," said Leslie, a new mother of three children. "The kids would say snotty things and John would stand by not wanting to get involved. He was afraid to hurt them and was so guilty that he had broken up a perfect home. Even if I was nice, the kids were still mean to me. They refused to do tasks and contributed nothing. Finally, I got so mad one day that I told them they could all pack their bags and live somewhere else. I also told John to start standing with me or he'd be standing alone. Funny thing, they finally got the message."

While it is important that the man and woman discuss the transition of new spouse from friend to stepparent with each other, it is just as important that they talk about it with the children. The children must understand that this new person who is coming into their lives will in fact be their parent. When everyone understands the process, compromise and agreements can be reached and problems avoided. Preventive medicine is always the best cure.

An underlying factor through all this process is the commitment of each spouse to the other's children. When a person marries, forming a stepfamily, he or she is marrying the spouse's children, too. The children cannot be separated from the spouse. Trying to do that only leads to hurt and turmoil.

Children require love, caring, and involvement from the adults in their lives. When a stepparent is unwilling to make a commitment to the children, the relationship will always be a struggling one. Further, the stepparent will find himself or herself in conflict between the spouse and the children. There will never be a zone of happiness, and the family will have difficulty achieving unity.

"Your" Versus "Mine"

The children in any marriage demand, and deserve, full commitment of the adults. Sometimes, the new parent prefers not to become involved. He or she may feel that the children will not accept him or her so why try. "They're just awful to me," may describe the situation aptly, but still an effort should be made to build a relationship with the stepchildren. Sometimes a stepparent must force himself or herself to build the relationship, but this is part of the responsibility that comes with being a parent in a stepfamily.

When Jim and Julie came for therapy, Julie disagreed with that premise. Even though Jim tried very hard to love her children, she rejected his offspring.

"They're like teenage vultures," she explained. "They come in and walk straight to the refrigerator. When I try to talk to them, they say you're not my mother. They are rude to my kids and I don't see why I have to take that abuse. If they want to see Jim, let them meet at a movie theater, or, better yet, a supermarket."

Jim and Julie did not realize that his children were playing the perfect game. They had stuck themselves between the two adults and were effectively breaking up the marriage. Both Jim and Julie had valid points, but the emotions involved in the issue prevented them from resolving it. Although the solution required some complex behavior, the premise was fairly simple. When the children came to visit, Jim had to set some expectations of appropriate behavior to which the children must adhere, or they could not visit. For her part, Julie had to engage in behaviors and activities that showed she cared for the children even if they rejected her.

Chapter 11   Dilemmas of the Stepparent

We believe that the "your" versus "mine" mentality as evidenced by Jim and Julie is the downfall of many stepfamilies. If spouses split the stepfamily with members taking sides, family unity is destroyed. The roles of the members of the stepfamily are so intertwined that if one persons pulls out of a relationship or refuses to accept the responsibilities of his or her role, chaos soon follows. Family life has developed and endured over the centuries because it is a force for survival. It can be the shelter and also the love reservoir from which family members can insure their sanity. If the family becomes disjointed, so do the family members.

Special Problems for the Male Stepparent

The role of the new parent can be confusing and the problems for the male and female stepparent are usually different. Their roles are often culturally or "courtroom" defined. The male is normally the person who moves into the stepfamily and assumes new children on a full-time basis. He may or may not have children of his own, and he may not have any skills as a parent. Even when he has children of his own, the experience he gained with them may not serve him well with the children of his new wife. Thus his role is extremely difficult, even with a wife who supports him entirely.

Like the lion who dominates the litter of cubs, the male must feel that he is in control and is needed. Sometimes when the very young are handled by others, animals will discard them because of their foreign smell. A similar analogy can be made for the male. Many messages will float through his head that push him toward withdrawal. Following are some of the more common ones:

1. These kids were raised by some other guy.
2. They walk, talk, and eat like him.
3. They do everything opposite of what I do.
4. Nobody ever says they look like me.
5. I'm living in a house of foreigners.
6. They don't respect me.
7. When will they ever start doing things the right way?

8. It's a hopeless battle. He tells them to do things one way and I tell them another.
9. They only look at me as a meal ticket.
10. My wife supports them and not me.

Along with these doubts, the male stepparent is frequently used to a different lifestyle. He must adapt to a new family, and that can be hard. This is often a time of deep misgiving as he wonders if he made the right decision.

The stepfamily needs a male adult, a person who is willing to sacrifice now for long-term payoffs or benefits. Sometimes this means the male may give love and receive little in return. Children will have difficulty adjusting to the idea of a new parent, especially in the beginning. Many of us want to be instant successes, but this seldom happens in the stepfamily, a point every male stepparent must learn.

The typical stepfamily takes time for its members to adjust to each other. If a family has lived a certain lifestyle for several years, it will take a year or longer to adjust to a new lifestyle. The male must understand that he must be a leader, but he must also expect defeat and false-starts along the way. When he loses, he must continue. Each victory, no matter how small, should be cherished.

Most of all, he must be willing to spend time with the children. This is particularly important when the children, or the male himself, do not want to be together. The adult must structure the time needed for the development of relationships even when the children are reluctant to accept him. The more one sees a face, the more he or she will grow to like it! The male can have a tremendous impact on the children if he is willing to take the first steps. He must believe that the children are his, and he should treat them as his own children. One of the greatest joys for the male is seeing that a child is starting to act like himself. Imitation truly is the highest form of flattery.

While the dynamics of the stepfamily itself can make it difficult for the male stepparent to gain the love and confidence of the children, society also hampers him. The stepfather is often reminded by others that these are not "his children," but the same folks will criticize him if he is remiss in his duties. In many cases, the children will not have the stepfather's last name, which can be embarrassing for both the children and the stepfather.

Chapter 11　　　　　　　　　　　Dilemmas of the Stepparent

Names are a point of contention in many stepfamilies. Many biological parents refuse to let their children use a different name, because they feel that this in some way implies that they are losing their children. This example of pride, however, often causes pain to the children. It is also sexist and favors males even when they are minimally involved with children.

One solution is to permit the children to use a dual identity. This is most practical in instances where the parents live a good distance from each other. The children can use the last name of the parent with whom they are staying. If they are with the non-custodial parent, that parent's last name would be used. When they are with the custodial parent, the custodial parent's last name would be used. This arrangement could be most effective for small children who develop strong attachments to both the biological and non-biological parent. When the child reaches an appropriate age, he or she could decide on a last name.

Some schools will do this if the parents ask them to. Unfortunately, this only works when all parents agree. A disagreeing parent can cause legal complications if a last name is used without permission. Still, we have seen the "portable" last name work for many children.

Special Problems for the Female Stepparent

While stepparents share many of the same problems, just like the man, the woman also faces some unique issues. In some cases she assumes the role of the full-time mother, but she may also be a part-time or weekend parent.

Because many men have trouble talking to their children, they usually plan activities in which they do not need to converse much. Trips to shopping malls, the movies, football games, and similar places are popular choices for the man who finds it difficult to keep a conversation going with his children.

When the stepmother is dragged along on such occasions, she should be made a normal part of the family. If the stepmother refuses, she seldom can be parent or friend, and seldom can build any type of relationship with the children. Though hard, it is beneficial for all family members when the stepmother assumes a positive role in the family.

Step by Step: A Guide to Stepfamily Living

We strongly believe that even weekend stepmothers can build positive relationships with the children. Following are some steps they can take:
1. Make rules that apply for the family all the time. What the children may do in some else's house is their business, but what they do in the stepmother's house is hers.
2. Give the weekend children a space to live. Make them feel a part of the family.
3. Give the weekend children some chores around the house and yard. Work can give one a feeling of belonging.
4. Keep in mind that all vacations lead to resentment by other family members, who may feel that the parents are playing favorites.
5. Call the children regularly just to say hello. Talking can help in building a relationship.

The stepmother should strive to create an atmosphere of acceptance. We have seen children fit in quite easily when they are made to feel welcome and comfortable. The most important thing is to make the children feel that they are important to both parents and that they belong. If the parent understands the child's needs, adjustment will be easier.

Stepparents, whether male or female, must realize that failure is a part of the process of developing unity. If one learns from his or her mistakes and leaves a path for change, the chances for family growth become greater. Success for the stepfamily means a functional family that provides emotional, psychological, and physical support for all family members.

We have no timetable to give. For some families the adjustment period takes months; for others it takes years. Most families adjust within a year or two. The success of the family ultimately falls to the husband and wife, and it remains up to them to take the steps that will determine the family's success.

Chapter 12
Preventing Friction in the Stepfamily

In almost every relationship the point is reached when people wonder whether they belong together. For members of stepfamilies, that point may be reached quite often as the family struggles for adjustment and attempts to build unity.

Some people say that once you have been divorced, breaking away from marriage is easier the next time. They cite the fact that some people get married three, four, five, or more times. The more often one has been divorced, the easier the process of divorce becomes.

We do not agree with this assumption, however. We believe that divorce is a painful process, one that most people do not want to repeat. People may fail at several marriages because they repeat the same lifestyle that led to divorce in the first place. They repeat the same problems. It is not that they find divorce easy; it is simply a matter of living emotionally unhealthy lives.

We recall one couple who had to get divorced in order to grow close to each other again. They had a classic love-hate relationship. When things were going good for them, they were in heaven. However, when things were bad, the fury between them was intense. They could not live with each other, but could not make it without the other person either. They would go along until they reached a severe crisis, and then they would divorce. A few months after the divorce, they would start dating again and soon thereafter they would remarry. This process went on for three or four cycles as their lives alternated between happiness and misery.

In our work, we have found many people who have said that if they worked as hard in their first marriage as they did in their second, they probably never would have gotten divorced. Because of statements like this, we are convinced that many people give a sincere effort to make their remarriage and stepfamily happy and successful.

This is not to say that keeping the romance going after a couple have been a part of a stepfamily for a time does not take some effort. It does. After a couple has passed the honeymoon stage and they start learning what each other is really like, it is normal for people to have second thoughts. Wondering if you did the right thing is common to everyone. When those thoughts become overwhelming, however, the stepfamily slips into trouble.

Reasons for Failure

We believe that marriages fail in stepfamilies for many reasons, but a few are far more common than others. Probably the greatest reason for failure is the lack of support within the relationship.

If either partner feels that the spouse is not entirely supportive, problems will soon brew. In a world where many people feel that they are not important, and suffer from the consequences of technology and huge conglomerates, it is vital that a person feels that someone believes in him or her. He or she must feel secure and believe that dreams can in fact become realities. If one spouse is constantly berating the other, arguing or fighting about silly, inconsequential matters, or pitting his or her mate against the children, the stepfamily will be plagued with tension and conflict. It will be virtually impossible to build unity. The members will not become a fully functioning family.

> *As a business executive, Phil made countless decisions that affected the lives of many people. However, in his family, Phil was in constant trouble. He disagreed with his wife, Pat, on how to raise the children and seemed to have little power as a new father. Each time he would ask the children to do something, they would either refuse or complain to their mother in attempts to avoid work. Phil and Pat argued constantly, and their relationship began to deteriorate. A result of this was that Phil became bored with his wife's conversation, because, in his opinion, it lacked the stimulation of his business encounters. Pat interpreted his growing inattention as a sign that he did not love her, and she put more of her time into the children's activities. As time passed, each of them spent more and more time apart—he at work and she with the children. It was no surprise that Phil eventually decided to leave.*

The husband and wife of a stepfamily must support each other completely and work together for the good of their family. When a husband and wife do not support each other, their relationship inevitably fails, with their marriage dissolving soon afterward.

Another source of failure of the marriage in a stepfamily is when the husband and wife confuse or misunderstand sex roles. Quite simply, when partners expect the spouse to do the work around the house, there will be trouble. The problem is worsened when the man and wife refuse to compromise because of "liberty" or "machismo."

When partners fall into this trap, every minor chore becomes a potential flashpoint for fighting. Partners may battle over each meal, the dishes, the vacuuming—the battlegrounds are unending. It may appear that each keeps a tally sheet of what he or she does and what the other does not do. Criticism is the typical mode of conversation as each person bluntly reminds the other of his or her inadequacies. Even when a chore is assumed by one partner, it is likely to be completed with resentment which only leads to more anger and bitterness. These couples often enter their marriage with unrealistic expectations and are unwilling to change their outlooks. Living in this kind of household can be torment.

Yet another major stumbling block to the success of the stepfamily is when the children become the main focus of the marriage. When a husband and wife find that their lives revolve around the children—wondering where they are, what activities they must be involved in, and planning every weekend around their needs—the couple should re-evaluate their relationship. When a couple and their needs become secondary to the needs of their children, they may have lost common adult interests. While children can be demanding, they should never overrule the couple's need for shared adult activities that will sustain their relationship long after the children are gone.

Bill and Sherry are an example of a couple that fits the above description. Married for 22 years, they had raised their two sons and a daughter quite admirably. When the trouble started, the youngest was finishing high school and the other two were in college. For years Sherry drove the children to all of their activities, while also helping in the grocery store that she and Bill owned. Bill also participated in activities with the boys, particularly in later years. This was rewarding for him and somewhat different since he had traveled extensively when the children were young and left much of the childrearing to Sherry.

Although they spent much time with their children, Bill and Sherry actually spent little time together. Over the years, they drifted apart from each other. Recently, they sold the grocery store and Sherry was starting a new career at a local bank. Bill had reached a managerial position in a small company, but his opportunity for advancement was limited. With their daughter leaving for college in several months, both Sherry and Bill wondered what was left for them.

They seemed to have little in common except the children, and the activities they each liked were quite different. During the last few months, Bill had been seeing another woman in her mid-thirties, who he claimed was "more alive." Not surprisingly, Bill and Sherry decided to separate to determine their feelings for each other.

Unquestionably, a couple that devotes themselves to their children will have little time for each other. They will deny themselves the chance to build a strong relationship that will endure after the children have grown and left home. Bill and Sherry found this out too late.

Sex is still another factor that can undermine and ruin the relationship between the husband and wife of a stepfamily. This is especially true when sexual activities are infrequent or judged to be inadequate by at least one spouse.

Everyone has a sex drive, which is a basic biological mechanism for survival. So strong and pervasive is this drive that problems that exist in a relationship often are manifest in the bedroom. When the sexual relationship is lacking in some way, so too is the caring of the couple. Sexual sharing is an intense way of loving someone and helps draw people closer. Sex can be a powerful bond.

We see numerous sexual problems. Some of the common ones include:

- The wife who abhors the experience but submits once weekly because she has to.
- The husband who has several extramarital affairs but cannot touch his wife.
- The man who talks of the great romantic life to friends, but is only "self-satisfying" in bed with his wife.
- The woman who still acts like a teenage virgin, and is unwilling to experiment because it is sinful. The "missionary position" is hard enough.
- The man or woman who demands a physically fit partner but can hardly fit on the bed.
- The man or woman who is constantly harassing the partner to look like a TV model.
- The man who insists his wife have sex whether or not she wants to.
- The spouse who does not want to interrupt TV because he or she is watching a good show.
- The spouse who reads a magazine article and believes that he or she and the mate are not having enough sex to meet national standards.

- The woman who refuses to understand her body, or is so ashamed that the room is as dark as a cave.
- The partner who demands orgasm as soon as he or she gets into bed.
- The man who can never express feelings, or can only say "I love you" after he has had intercourse.

A sexual problem means a relationship problem. It affects all aspects of the marriage. Trying to hide it does not work, nor does avoiding the problem minimize it. The only way to solve an issue is to admit the problem and then face it. When a couple is unable to solve the problem themselves, they must seek competent help.

Sometimes seeking help can be difficult, however. Carla, for example, came to counseling with problems in sex and her relationship.

"Hal and I have been experiencing difficulties for over 10 years in our marriage," she said. *"He's a premature ejaculator and sex is very unsatisfying for me. Besides that, we argue most of the time. It seems like we have sex as if we are on a clock. Certain days of the week and specific times are designated, and we can't seem to get out of the pattern. I can just tell by the way he acts that I'm supposed to give in.*

"Well, lately I haven't been so willing. I've asked him to go to a specialist but he won't do it. He went to our family doctor about seven years ago and he was told that he had a mild case of diabetes. The doctor said this could affect his sex life. Well, that was all he needed. He said he couldn't do anything about it and that was that. To tell you the truth, I just don't see it that way. I have set up appointments for him to see a specialist or a urologist, and he seems to avoid going by creating all sorts of excuses. Finally, I read that therapists could help with some sexual difficulties so I made an appointment, but he still refuses to go and talk about it. He says it's my problem. I guess he's right. My problem is him."

Hal and Carla are typical of couples where one partner is willing to seek help to find a solution to a problem, but the other is not. Not seeking the necessary help, however, only makes the problem worse.

Chapter 12 Preventing Friction in the Stepfamily

For some couples, the problem is not so specific. The romance may be just disappearing, each day falling into a routine of sameness. A lack of romance often is equated with a lack of caring.

To keep a marriage alive and vital, romance must be an integral part of the relationship. Too many people begin to take a spouse for granted, an act that soon weakens the relationship. Unexpected vacations, giving unannounced affection or gifts, playfulness, laughter, and similar things help keep the romance and thrill between two people. They are all necessary to avoid falling into the traps that can lead to the failure of a marriage.

The Second Time Around

Besides all these points, it is important to remember that most spouses of stepfamilies are trying marriage for the second time. They usually have memories of the first spouse and that past life must be dealt with and put to rest. The ghosts must be exorcised.

For some people, even though their previous spouse left them desperately sad and confused, they search for and find a new partner with traits remarkably similar to the ex. These people inevitably wind up in the same types of struggles, confront the same problems, and grapple with the same doubts that they thought they left behind. It is like the replaying of an old movie. But just like that old movie in which one knows the script, the familiar arguments and disagreements that the individual faces are harder to take the second time around. Patience is limited. When we counsel people who are experiencing this problem, we tell them that they must share part of the blame. After all, they picked their new spouses.

Mike's first wife was controlling and nagging. She was the kind of woman one would prefer to leave rather than talk to or discuss a problem with. His new wife was non-controlling until about six months into the marriage. The change in her behavior was gradual, and Mike did not notice the changes.

At first she started calling him if he was late from work. Soon she became afraid that he was with another woman. The marriage was becoming strained, because most of the real messages were not being communicated. His wife's greatest fear was that he would leave her, because he had done this once already—he had left his first wife for her. This time, according to her reasoning, he might leave her.

Mike added to his wife's fears by commenting on how nice other women looked, and he often acted as if his wife was not up to his standards. She came to believe that she could never satisfy him, so her only recourse was to make sure that he never had a chance to see anybody else. She sought to control his time and movements.

Mike could not understand his wife's motivations, but he had become quite aware of her suffocating behavior toward him. As she sought more control, he pushed for more freedom. It was not long before they were locked in a power battle from which there was no escape. Mike felt that he needed some space. He was receiving too much affection, and also sensed the desperate feelings of insecurity from his spouse because she was afraid. He found these messages to be confusing and conflicting, and could not explain what was happening.

As the problem worsened, Mike eventually turned away from his wife. He rejected all parts of her behavior, and was soon on the way to another divorce.

Clearly, recognition of past patterns of behavior can help people deal with those behaviors in the present and future. For Mike and his spouse, new behaviors were in order for both of them. We strongly believe that for any relationship to last, both partners must work hard at it.

A frightening realization for people like Mike is that when they sense their new marriage faltering, they want to end it before it hurts too much. Burned badly once, they do not want to be burned again. Many people stay in first marriages far longer than they should. Unfortunately, this can cause repercussions in the second marriage. Rather than risking the hurt, they prefer to run away from it. By not risking, however, they may not be giving the new marriage a chance.

Some people desire and expect the depth and richness of a ten-year relationship in just six months. This seldom happens. Part of the growth of any relationship comes through sticking through the hard times and making a "go" of it. When an individual finds the same problems in his or her second marriage that were in the first, he or she should examine himself or herself before condemning the new spouse. Often the individual is at least an equal part of the cause of the problem, and sometimes the major cause. It is human nature to blame problems on others—jobs, bosses, the children, and, of course, the spouse. Casting blame, however, does little to solve problems.

For any problem to be solved, the true cause must be identified. If that cause falls to the individual, he or she must be willing to make the necessary changes. If it is because of the spouse, the spouse needs to be made aware of the problem, and helped to bring about the change in behavior that will alleviate it.

Some individuals forget that their spouses may be reacting to the relationship in the best way they can. For many couples, solving problems requires that both people alter their behavior. Husband and wife must work as a team in making their marriage a success.

Introspection of the past is usually helpful. Besides the memories and lifestyle shared with the ex-spouse, one brings his or her children, brothers, sisters, and parents into the new relationship. While children certainly can demand much time, brothers and sisters can offer helpful or harmful advice, it is the influence of one's parents that can affect a new marriage in a significant way. After all, a person's parents were the ones that taught him or her "how to behave" in marriage, "how to love," and "how to parent." If one's parents were inadequate role models, it is probable that the individual will have trouble in assuming his or her own role in a family. Such people must work hard to overcome past family habits or messages if they are to avoid the problems their own family suffered.

It is always worthwhile for a husband and wife to share the memories and messages of their families with each other. Such discussions can often cast a helpful light on current problems. Some of the topics or issues a couple should ask each other include:

Step by Step: A Guide to Stepfamily Living

1. Describe your relatives. Were any of them a bit odd?
2. How was love shown in your family?
3. Describe your relationships with your brothers and sisters.
4. Describe your first memory as a child.
5. Are most of your memories good or bad? Describe the best of each.
6. Describe your mother and father.
7. Who was the stronger parent? In what ways?
8. Describe the men in your family, and then the women.
9. Who was the boss of the family?
10. How were conflicts resolved by your parents?
11. What were the major areas of disagreement between your parents?
12. How did each of your parents deal with your ex-spouse's personality?

In discussing these and other questions, it is important to remember that even if the marriage of your parents was a successful one, they were people of a past generation. Their world was a different one. While some of the pressures and stresses that they had to cope with were the same as couples today because much of the human condition remains constant, many were different. For example, it is unlikely that they had to deal with high technology, decay of the inner cities, the effects of the sexual revolution, or the high rate of crime or drugs. Their outlook on life may have been different, and their techniques for a successful marriage may not work so well today. The types of conflicts modern couples face are quite different than those faced by couples of the past.

Chapter 12   Preventing Friction in the Stepfamily

Ingredients for Success

If there are any ingredients for keeping a marriage healthy and successful, they are the faith a husband and wife have in each other, their willingness to compromise, and their ability to communicate. Without these factors in a relationship, it is difficult for people to stay together.

Faith is the foundation of a marriage. Its essence is composed of the acceptance of each other by partners. It means taking the other person as he or she is, and being willing to let that person change and grow at his or her own pace. Just because an individual wants his or her spouse to behave in a certain way does not insure that person will. Too often people enter into a relationship believing that they can mold their spouse into the person they truly want to marry. This may sound silly, but it happens again and again. A person can be sloppy, or not be willing to help around the house before the marriage, and the behavior is accepted. "Well, that's just the way he is" is the typical excuse. While the behavior is accepted before marriage, it seldom is afterward. Suddenly, the new spouse is expected to change the way he or she has been acting all along. The point here is a simple one: When spouses accept each other for what each other truly is, the chances for a successful marriage increase.

When we talk about compromise, we are not advocating one spouse pushing the other to agreement. Rather, it means a frank discussion and willingness on the parts of both partners to give up some things for the benefit of the marriage. Certainly we do not mean one must compromise integrity, but neither do we mean one may continue to act stubbornly. Marriage is best characterized as a give-and-take. The more one gives to the relationship, the more he or she is likely to receive.

Communication is no less important than faith and compromise. True communication requires sitting down and discussing both problems and happy times in a relatively calm, easy tone. Arguments lead nowhere and accomplish little except hurt feelings. Communication is the vital core of any relationship. If one does not permit others into his or her life, he or she cannot expect them to understand his or her feelings and needs.

We believe that it is good to share what happens in our daily lives, no matter how mundane the topics may be. Setting time aside each day for discussion, sharing, and communication adds excitement to a marriage. It builds a bond; it strengthens a sense of unity, giving husband and wife a feeling of "we-ness."

Without good communication, partners may begin to slip away from each other. Without daily contact, they can lose focus. Without sharing, they can lose each other.

Chapter 13
Creating a Family Atmosphere

Most parents find that the creation of a family atmosphere and the disciplining of children are difficult and inseparable. The parents in stepfamilies are no exception to this rule. Indeed, because of the added pressures on building and maintaining the unity of a stepfamily, the job can be even harder.

In our culture parents are crucial to the security of children, who, at the very least, depend on their parents for love and the development of their self-concepts. When a marriage ends and children suffer through the anguish of divorce, they may have trouble growing close to their parents again, especially to the stepparent. Burned once, children become cautious. This wariness can cause a gap in the relationships between the members of the stepfamily, leading to disharmony and confused feelings.

Step by Step: A Guide to Stepfamily Living

The parents in a stepfamily must cope with a variety of problems if they are to be effective in their roles. One of the most common problems is discipline. Usually, in the traditional couple, one parent is stricter than the other. Over a period of time, however, a system of childrearing and discipline evolves in which each partner begins to accept the other's opinions. A compromise eventually is reached.

In the stepfamily, in instances where the stepparent is viewed as a threat, compromise may not be easily achieved. Here is a typical example. The non-biological father attempts to discipline the children, but his rules and style are different than the children's biological father. Moreover, the children resent their new father who they blame for having hurt them and ruined their mother's marriage. This situation is worsened when the mother does not agree with her new husband's methods of punishment. Although she wants help with discipline, she wants to control the amount and manner. The results of such scenarios are frequent and serious arguments that ensue can rock the foundation of the new family.

Fortunately, battles like this can be avoided before causing pain. First, the parents of a stepfamily must realize that they do not have the luxury of developing a parenting style like traditional couples, but rather plunge right into a relationship with children.

> *Juan and Mary could never agree on discipline, and always seemed to be on the opposite side of every issue. Juan had high expectations for the children, and believed that hard work was the only sure way to achieve success. Mary thought that life was full of happiness and that one should limit work as much as possible and seek excitement instead. The children were in the middle, never certain of what path to follow. The messages they received from their parents were contradictory, and they usually ended up doing what they wanted, though they seldom felt good about their decisions.*

> *Juan and Mary's disagreements were aggravated when the children started manipulating them. The entire family became involved over the issue of discipline, and the arguments between the parents worsened. Eventually, Juan and Mary fought so much that they decided to end their marriage.*

Chapter 13 — Creating a Family Atmosphere

At the root of discipline is love, and this can be an area of strong conflict for the remarried couple. Many stepparents feel guilty about the past relationship and leaving children behind. They have trouble getting close to the new children. They may not be able to show warmth and love, because of hidden anger at not being able to give their own children the same amount of time and consideration. The stepchildren may also have trouble coping with their anger, and instead of expressing it toward the biological parent, may direct it at the new parent if for no other reason than he or she is an easier target. For most couples discussing and understanding these negative feelings in an open and constructive manner is the best way to overcome them.

When Charlotte came for counseling, she believed that the problems in her family were all her fault. No matter how hard she tried, her stepchildren never liked her. In trying to understand the overall situation, we noticed that some problems had little to do with Charlotte. Several years before the remarriage, the children's original mother had left because she could not stand the strain of the marriage. Claiming economic pressures, she left the children with their father. Recently, she had moved back to the area and sought to re-establish herself with her children.

The children were confused and angry by their mother's actions. Not wanting to antagonize her for the fear that she would go away again, they blamed their problems on Charlotte who received the brunt of their anger.

In an attempt to ease their guilt over their behavior, the children made their mother perfect and picked on every fault of Charlotte. It was not until these issues were discussed at a family meeting that Charlotte realized what was actually happening. Understanding the problem fully enabled her to point out the unfairness of the situation and encouraged her husband to stand by her when facts were distorted.

By working together she and her husband were able to take control of their family. They were able to begin creating a family atmosphere.

The Importance of Discipline

We believe that discipline is a key to the success of any family, and is at the heart of family atmosphere. When fair and consistent consequences for behavior are established, children know what is expected of them. They also know what will happen if they do not abide by the rules. Alfred Adler, a famous psychotherapist stated an important principle when he said, "Discipline is the seed from which freedom grows."

The following example illustrates this point.

Suppose a large group came to a beautiful resort. They were lying around a pool and the hotel manager came out to meet everyone. She stated that the members of the group could take part in various activities, including swimming, fishing, tennis, badminton, golf, and sailing. When she was done, all the group members, except Johnny, went off to participate in the activities of their choice. Johnny remained sitting by the pool. He had never learned how to do anything other than swim, and so he could do nothing else during his vacation. He had not acquired the discipline that would have helped him be free. The lack of discipline limited his freedom to choose.

Many parents do this very thing with their children. Unwittingly, by not providing discipline, they deny their children the freedom to achieve their greatest personal growth.

Sometimes, parents permit just about anything in the name of "freedom." Children are allowed to do whatever they wish. This, however, is not freedom, but anarchy. When each individual of the stepfamily does only what he or she pleases, then each person is concerned only with self-interest and does not learn to help or care for others.

If a family is a family, then everyone must share in it. For example, we believe that everyone in a family should help with chores rather than leave them for one person (usually the mother!). We also feel that paying children for doing chores gives them money in the wrong way. Such an act gives children a distorted value that every task in life deserves a payment, but this is not a balanced representation of life. Chores are a part of everyday living and children need to learn that they will be doing

Chapter 13   Creating a Family Atmosphere

them all their lives. Expecting a reward for something as basic as a chore will lead to a bitter realization when that child becomes an adult.

Without question, effective parenting has become more difficult during the last 10 to 15 years. Our society has experienced significant changes and children no longer respond to the dominant-submissive relationship which was typical of the parent-child relationship of the past.

Children today seek more democratic involvement with equality and participation in their families than their own parents did. They see examples of democracy, equality, and participation on TV, in school, in political campaigns, and, hopefully, in their parents. When each person in a family is treated with respect, when each person has a vital role within the family, family members, at the least, will enjoy peaceful coexistence.

Unfortunately, the parents of stepfamilies, because they are thrust into being the parents of children they hardly know, may not always understand this. Sally is a good example.

The new mother of twelve-year-old Tommy, she thought that parents must be bosses and that she should never let her "guard" down or she would lose control of Tommy. From the start she made sure that Tommy did everything correctly. It was as if Sally was scared that since this was not her biological son he would take advantage of her. Through all this Tommy appeared confused and resentful that he did all the right things but received little acknowledgment. If he balked at following Sally's orders, he was severely scolded. Sally imposed the rules, but was afraid to get close to her new son.

The situation was complicated by the sudden appearance of Sally's fifteen-year-old son, Louis, who had decided to come and live with his mother. Because of her need not to upset Louis or drive him away, Sally allowed him to live in her house under an entirely different set of rules.

This, quite naturally, created a crisis in the family as Tommy resented Louis's freedom and both boys fought over Sally's love. It was during this turmoil that Sally realized she needed a more even-handed approach where both boys learned discipline and yet received an adequate and equal amount of love.

Children are social beings and want to belong. Misbehavior in fact is usually a way of being a part of the family. All behavior has a purpose and sometimes the child wishes to be significant in the family but he or she does not know how to do this. Breaking the rules gets a response. While establishing a caring environment is essential to reducing misbehavior, we have found that there are several other steps families can take to encourage children to follow the rules:

1. Parents must remember that even though children are not equal in size, life experiences, or intelligence, they deserve equal respect.
2. A person is not a victim of forces beyond his or her control. Everyone makes choices. Because a child is in a stepfamily does not mean that he or she is supposed to misbehave. "Not" making a decision is still a decision.
3. Children need to be a part of the family. Doing everything for children denies them the chance to gain vital problem-solving skills, and teaches them that all problems will be solved by their parents. Picking up a child's clothes merely teaches the child that his or her parents are servants.
4. Parents should let children be a part of both the fun and work of the family. Children can help plan vacations and do chores. Hard work teaches resourcefulness.
5. Children need to learn freedom along with responsibility. Letting children do whatever they want leads to chaos. Many of our problem adolescents have no respect for anyone but themselves and their peers. They have been taught selfishness, not responsibility.
6. Encouragement, not criticism, is the key to a family's success.
7. Children can be taught to get along with and respect their brothers and sisters. Not only must parents teach this; they must live it.
8. Nagging, preaching, and repeating directions are useless activities and contribute to misbehavior. The old axiom, "Actions speak louder than words," is true. Parents must be consistent in their expectations and rules, and follow the rules themselves.

9. The final decision on any major issue rests with the parents. Children must have limits and rules. If the parents are unwilling to fulfill their role as parents, no one else will.
10. Competition makes enemies of every fellow human. Competitive children strive for success because they believe only in themselves and do not care what others are doing. Children need to learn to cooperate and not compete in the family.

Of course, reading what to do is much simpler than knowing how to do it. Still, parents have a large part in a family's success and taking the above steps can help guarantee a happier and more successful family.

Help and Punishment

Over the years we have seen again and again that guiding and helping a child is much more effective in changing inappropriate behavior than punishment. Parents who show their children how to become involved with the family and support them in their mistakes as well as successes usually have capable and well-behaved children.

Many parents are too critical of their children. They have forgotten that making mistakes is a part of learning. Adults are often so perfection-oriented that they want to be good at everything, even if they have never done it before, and they want their children to be the same way. But when they impose such strict standards on their children, everyone usually ends up frustrated.

These parents would be wiser to give their children a new task, help them with it, but let the children do most of the work. After the children have learned the skills, let them experiment. True, they might break a few things—there might be some false starts and outright mini-disasters—but the children will gain important skills and grow in self-confidence.

All of us like responsibility. Adults like to be given the opportunity on the job to show their talents and feel good about themselves. Children deserve the same chance. They should be encouraged for their talents and initiative. Many great people have suffered failure on their way to greatness. Why deny children that same road?

Besides strong encouragement and support, children should be made a part of the stepfamily, the horizon open to them so that they can achieve their highest potentials. Most people can give in to laziness, and parents should be willing to push their children when necessary. If children learn to contribute to the family from the beginning, they will be more likely to continue to do so as they get older.

Parents must explain to the children that everyone must contribute to the family or everyone suffers. If a child refuses to perform a task, a suitable consequence should be determined. Consequences should never be physical punishment or excessive verbiage. We believe that all children misbehave, and usually a reprimand or discussion will stop the action from occurring in the future.

When misbehavior becomes a consistent and serious problem, stronger measures must be taken. A series of logical consequences must be laid out. First, the parents must sit down with the child, and examine the action and what harm it is causing to the child and others. Next, the child must be informed that if the action continues, certain consequences will occur. These consequences should fit the action. When the misbehavior occurs again, the parents recognize the action and employ the consequences. At this point, little further discussion should be undertaken and arguments should be avoided. After all, what is left to discuss? The misbehavior and consequences were discussed previously, and the action of the parents is simply the logical step.

Here is an illustration of what we mean by a logical consequence.

Johnny had trouble feeding his dog. He never would fill the bowl, leaving the chore to his mother. A simple consequence stopped this misbehavior. Johnny was told that dogs need to eat just like people or they will die. If Johnny forgot to feed the dog, he would not get dinner either. Of course, he tested his mother, but she would not budge from the consequence. She did not argue with him or lecture him once more how dogs need to eat and that the dog was his pet. She simply did not give Johnny his dinner, nor did he receive a snack later when he cried that he was hungry. Within three days, he was feeding the dog regularly and had learned two valuable lessons: It is not acceptable to starve animals, and if one wants a pet, he or she must take care of it.

The strategy of logical consequence can be applied to countless problems. The key is for the parents to agree on the consequences and then stick together. If the child can play one parent against the other, any attempts of changing the child's behavior are likely to fail.

The Parents as Models

The modeling of the parents can teach important values to the children. A couple that belittles, criticizes, and complains teaches these negative behaviors to their children. Partners must show caring, love, and respect; they should be willing to help each other and praise each other's actions. Conflicts should be managed constructively and with a sense of humor. Parents should maintain positive attitudes and encourage group discussions of important family matters. In our world of tension and stress, this can be hard to do, but it is essential to the strength and success of the stepfamily.

Parents should never force their children into the role of servant. Here is a typical example.

The mother and father are entertaining friends at home. The older daughter is expected to watch her younger brother. When the boy's bedtime passes and he becomes bothersome, the father orders his daughter to amuse her brother. She does so, but with a sigh of regret and the kindling of resentment.

The father's request here was unreasonable. It was the duty of the parents to see that the young son was put to bed. The father took advantage of his daughter.

Rudolph Dreikurs, in a book entitled *Discipline Without Tears,* provides some important behaviors and clues to success in a family. He offers parents the following suggestions:

1. Avoid discouragement. Work for improvement, not perfection.
2. Commend effort and build on strengths.
3. Separate the "action done" from the doer. Because children do something wrong does not mean they are bad children.

4. Failure is not one's worth but one's lack of skill. Show faith.
5. Let a child move at his or her own speed. Stimulate, do not push.
6. Integrate the child into the family.
7. Do not praise. Some children only work for this special recognition. Encourage. Let the children take credit for their successes. Encouragement builds a strong self-concept.
8. Give opportunities to the discouraged child, not just to those who are responsible.
9. Solicit the help of family members with a misbehaving child.
10. Be optimistic.

Even with these tips for helping a family become closer, the process of family growth takes time. Family members need to learn to treat each other with respect and as they themselves wish to be treated. It is hard for us not to like someone who likes us. Such steps plant the seeds of love in a family.

Often children will have trouble getting close to a new parent, and strokes of affection may be few. Even if they do get close, they may experience a powerful negative reaction shortly thereafter. It is not unusual for a child to laugh and play with a stepparent and a few minutes later announce, "You're not my real parent." Certainly, this hurts the parent's feelings, but it is easier to understand when he or she realizes how the child is struggling with conflicting emotions.

> As a new mother, Susan was having trouble keeping Brenda under control. Whenever she went to the supermarket, she would leave Brenda in the car so that she could have an easier time of shopping. Susan would tell Brenda that she would bring her a present.
>
> Soon Brenda began to realize the effects of "bribing" and demanded material offerings as a reward for being good. Susan forgot that if you bribe a child for good behavior, you are showing that you do not trust the child and are actually discouraging her.

Most children have a desire to belong and contribute to their families, and want to be good. They want to be accepted. However, children need to see the advantages of cooperating and being part of a family rather than asking, "What's in it for me?" Soon the appetite of material gain grows monstrous, and a child believes the world owes him or her everything. If the child does not get what he or she wants, he will punish others. "I'll show them!" As parents reward children with material things, they deny them the basic satisfactions of living and how to contribute and be useful in our world.

Unity in the Stepfamily

It is crucial for any stepfamily to forget the past and begin working on their own memories. Family members should take trips together, go fishing, watch movies, make puzzles, and do a hundred other things that bring enjoyment and result in happy memories. Sitting before a TV screen night after night does little to promote family unity. Sharing does. Parents should share in their children's activities, go to their special, and "not so special," events. Parents should be with their children to share their miseries and their joys.

It is not hard to compile a list of activities in which sharing is made easy. Here are just a few:

1. Do housecleaning together and celebrate afterward.
2. The children can take their parents out to dinner. (The parents may give them the money beforehand.)
3. Families should eat meals together, especially dinner. This time should be used to communicate and share. Many troubled families never share a meal and never share of themselves. They feel uneasy sitting together.
4. Families should play games and do a variety of activities together. Football, badminton, hiking, picnicking, and monopoly are some suggestions.
5. Parents should find out what their children do in school. They should read the reports and papers of their children.
6. Parents should share their work and themselves with their children.

Establishing a philosophy of family is not easy. Developing an open atmosphere where concerns can be aired and dealt with without criticism is hard for most of us and takes a lot of work. The parents in stepfamilies often feel doubly-burdened. Because their previous marriage failed, they place enormous pressure on themselves to do it right this time. Without understanding the reasons for the problems of the earlier marriage, however, they may continue the same old patterns with the results being the same.

Understanding, modeling, teaching, involvement, caring, and encouragement are the most effective tools for the success of any stepfamily. It has been our experience that families who rely on them are more successful than those that do not.

Chapter 14
Understanding Children's Behavior in the Stepfamily

Raising a child in any family is difficult and the stepfamily is no exception. Most parents want to teach their children self-discipline, but often the behavior of the adults reinforces dependence and self-gratification in the child rather than self-reliance.

Most children are far smarter than their parents believe. Children generally react to how they view a situation, their behavior a reflection of their perceptions. In this chapter we will explore why children exhibit certain negative behaviors, and what parents can do to eliminate them.

An individual can influence another's behavior, but only under extreme circumstances can he or she control another's attitudes and actions. We like to point out that the only guaranteed way to get others to do what you want is to put a gun to their head, and even then some people will strongly resist. The best way for parents to affect the behavior of their children is by providing solid examples of acceptable behavior. When honesty is a part of a parent's behavior, it is likely his or her children will be honest. When a parent lies regularly, however, how can one expect his or her children to tell the truth?

Children respond to the behavior of their parents. Whenever parents alter their behavior, the changes offer new avenues of behavior to their children. If a boy does something wrong and his father berates him for it, only to see the boy do the same thing again tomorrow, clearly a change in the father's behavior is warranted. Thus, if a child is not cooperating no matter how much his or her parent lectures, begs, or punishes, then the parent's action is probably contributing to the negative behavior.

Unfortunately, when confronted with such situations, few parents know what to do next. Exhausting what they consider to be all of their possibilities, some parents resort to physical force. But this is seldom the answer either.

In our clinical practice we have noted that parents seem to be experiencing more trouble with their children these days, and that parents are becoming increasingly upset. It seems that the old ways of raising children do not work anymore, and that successful traditions for childrearing are being ignored.

Many people complain that the behavior of children in our society is deplorable. Children today are noisy, inconsiderate, and unmannerly. They often show disrespect for parents and other adults and may actually insult them. It is not unusual to see children misbehave in public places by crying, having temper tantrums, demanding special treats, and constantly asking for money. Parents plead, punish, and bribe to gain some tranquility. How have these changes developed?

Chapter 14　　　　　　　Understanding Children's Behavior

The Changing American Society

Some child experts believe that democracy, as a way of life for Americans, has brought about significant openness and change in our society. While this change has been evolving through the entire history of our country, it has been speeded by the tremendous impact of the Information Age. Electronics—TV, radio, telephones, computers, stereos, CDs and VCRs—have spread information to every part of the land. The Information Age has broken down taboos and made people aware of alternate lifestyles. A hundred years ago, rather than being played on the six o'clock news, the protest marches of the sixties would have remained isolated incidences.

The issue of equality has also grown in stature. One need only consider the Civil Rights Movement, ERA, and the battles for gay rights and the homeless to realize the power of the concept of equality.

Americans on the whole believe in equality, and this has transformed not only our society, but our parenting patterns. Everyone has a chance and nobody "rules" over anyone. It used to be that the father dominated the whole family. This is seldom the case anymore. Decisions that in the past belonged solely to the father now are made jointly with the mother. Children are increasingly asked their opinions. In many cases, authoritarian fathers are overruled and rightfully sabotaged by other family members.

The push for equality has occurred in virtually every area of our society—government, labor, sex, race, and ethnicity, as well as in the family. Yet, while they are quite willing to accept the idea of equality in the workplace, many parents are unwilling to accept it in their families. As parents, they wish to be superior and cling to the "you-do-as-I-say" philosophy even though they know it is ineffective. Exposed to democratic ideals in school, on TV, and with their friends, children are maturing faster, know more, and have more experience than their parents may realize. A child in a stepfamily may live through situations and be forced to cope with emotions that will mature him or her far beyond his or her peers.

Neil Kalter, in his book *Growing Up With Divorce*, points out that society has changed its fundamental attitudes toward children. Rather than protecting children from life's troubles, parents are preparing them for the struggle. This ideology focuses on the belief that children must be exposed early to adult experiences so that they may be ready for the cruel world.

This attitude, however, in our opinion, only makes a child's life more difficult, confusing, and pushes children beyond their developmental abilities. There are many cultural factors that can contribute to making childrearing difficult today including:

1. The rising divorce rate and emergence of the nontraditional family.
2. Poor economic conditions which have caused single parents to struggle for survival and children to work.
3. Dual-career families and the decrease in available family time.
4. The advent of TV, which often becomes a passive babysitter for parents and a distributor of uncensored material for children.
5. The availability of drugs and the ability to buy them.
6. A sexually-oriented society that preoccupies itself with constant titillation and encourages experimentation at a young age.

Some experts worry that children cannot handle the problems they encounter these days and suggest that today's children need to be more sheltered. Indeed, children seem to desire more adult-like activities, yet still appear to have trouble assuming responsibility.

Defining what limits and experiences are important for a child are vitally important for the parents in a stepfamily. This child will likely be forced to deal with powerful emotions and situations for which he or she has little experience. Coping with divorce, befriending confused parents, and assuming adult roles in a single-parent family may be but a few of the circumstances that can separate this child from peers.

While these experiences can widen the psychological and emotional scope and maturity of a child, they can also be damaging, and it is important that parents provide the necessary support and protection. Parents must assume the burden when it becomes too heavy, and enable the child to cope with the experiences as he or she can handle them. We suggest that parents remember what they were like at 6, 8, 12 or 15 years of age, and from that reasonably judge how much pressure their own children can manage.

Parents cannot always change the experiences that a child will have during divorce or in a stepfamily, but the parent can lessen some of the conflict and pain. Parents should always be mindful of the child's needs, and not make thoughtless assumptions of how a child will react to a given problem.

Parents, for example, should not assume that a child must be made aware of everything that is occurring in the family. The process of divorce and remarriage can be overwhelming to children. Yet, we find parents who believe that a child must experience and hear everything that is happening so that he or she has no questions or doubts. This parent will haul a child to divorce court to witness the process, or explain how every piece of furniture was divided. Others will involve their children in long custody battles and expect the relationship to revert to normal afterward. They think they are relieving doubt, confusion and fear, when in fact they are usually causing it.

At the other extreme are those parents who expect their children to act like adults. They believe that if they explain "things" their children will understand. These parents cannot comprehend why, after explaining to a six-year-old girl that she should hug her new father, the girl cries and backs away. The child simply needs time. The parents must be willing to give her that time to adjust to her new life.

Balancing Equality with Responsibility

Equality and responsibility must always be balanced within a positive family atmosphere. Some people like to think that democracy means freedom, and they interpret that to mean they can do whatever they wish. Democracy does mean freedom, but it implies respect for others. Democracy without respect leads to anarchy.

Democracy, therefore, implies a sense of order which entails restrictions, obligations, and responsibilities. This order provides benefits for everyone. Too often parents permit their children to have freedom, but require of them no responsibility. Children then lose a sense of self, of right and wrong, and do not learn how to live in a democratic society. With structured limits, a child develops a sense of security and worth; without them, children become spoiled.

One of the most important tasks of parents is to stimulate and encourage children into being a part of society and the human race without demanding submission and forcing compliance. To do this, certain principles must be understood:

1. Children want to belong. Even if a child misbehaves, he or she still wants to be a part of the family group. From their successes, children learn how to behave. A child will try many methods to achieve a sense of "belonging."

2. Behavior is goal-directed. Right or wrong, a child will do what gives him or her a place, and will abandon behavior that makes him or her feel left out or separate. How children think they belong and what behavior they do to achieve that goal may not always be understood by either child or parent.

3. Children are excellent observers but erratic interpreters. They often draw incorrect conclusions and thus pick incorrect behavior to win their places.

   Joan was happy when she learned that she would have a baby sister with whom to live and play. She quickly volunteered to help her mother take care of the baby, but her mother refused Joan's offer. Not long after the baby arrived, Joan realized that her mother was giving her new sister all the attention. After a few weeks, Joan began to "copy" the baby's behaviors and

Chapter 14　　　　　　Understanding Children's Behavior

would soil her clothes and even stage tantrums. Of course Joan received attention, but not what she expected. However, punishment was better than no attention at all.

4. A child's environment prepares him or her for life's accomplishments and difficulties. Sometimes a child with a handicap will become highly successful while his or her "normal" peers give up in face of life's struggles. How can we explain this?

   While there can be no single answer the answers to success and achievement can be found collectively in the family atmosphere. Children absorb the basic values and morals of their family. When parents are understanding and tolerant of others, their children usually are, too. When parents nurture their children, support and encourage them, the children most often become successful adults.

   The relationship of the parents becomes the model for all the relationships in the family. If the parents stress cooperation, this, rather than competition, will be a pervading feeling in the family. If the parents are hostile and strive to overpower each other, the children will attempt to overpower each other. When the children share a common trait, this trait frequently reveals the general family atmosphere.

5. Equally important is the positioning of the children in the stepfamily. Common in most families, but particularly true of stepfamilies, each child vies for a position, a situation made more complex when new children are added. Not only must a child contend with his siblings but now he or she must compete with stepbrothers and stepsisters.

   Larry, a twelve-year-old and the firstborn of the family, enjoyed his role as the leader of the children and took pride in being the perfect child. He set the standards and the rest of the children had to live up to them. When his father remarried, his new wife, Evelyn, brought her three teenagers to the family. Suddenly Larry was fourth in line and he resented it. In an attempt to assume dominance, he bossed his brothers and sisters but they resisted. To gain eventually began experimenting with drugs.

Larry's problems began when he was bumped from his role of eldest to being a middle child. Typically, middle children have difficulty competing with older siblings because their older brothers or sisters have more experiences. Younger children may become spoiled or helpless as others "wait" on them. For after all, they are the youngest and often become the center of attention. Understanding the implications of a child's position in the family can be advantageous to parents as they try to build a positive family atmosphere.

6. Encouragement rather than discouragement is the most useful parenting technique. In our opinion, a child who displays maladaptive behavior is doing so out of discouragement. Children who believe that they are failures and doubt their abilities are our problem children. We are always saddened that some stepfamilies give up on their children. Before doing that, parents must try to see things from the child's perspective.

Perhaps the child's negative behavior is a result of anger over the divorce, feeling ignored by a parent, or believing that he or she is second rate in the new family. In a tragic twist, such suspicions are often confirmed by a parent's continued focus on the negative.

Far too many parents fail to recognize and encourage their children. Even our society is negatively-oriented. Our newspapers and TV shows talk about what is wrong with our world, but offer little suggestion for improvement. When we do workshops, we ask people to list ten positive and ten negative facts about our society. The negative list is quickly finished, but people flounder on the positive one. The same thing happens when we ask couples to describe the worse and best things about their mates and their children.

Parents should always focus on the positive with their children. They should encourage their children toward independence with an attitude that says, "You will make it and you're okay with me." If a child fails, parents should urge him or her to try again, and offer techniques that can help bring about success. Parents should help a child build skills on his or her strengths, while at the same time working on improving the weaknesses.

Chapter 14 Understanding Children's Behavior

In his book *Adlerian Counseling*, Dr. Tom Sweeney explains that cooperation, not conformity, should be the goal between parents and children. Children need to participate in the labors of daily living. Sometimes parents ignore this by doing everything for the child or by assigning tasks to a youngster that they would not do themselves. Dr. Sweeney offers six additional guidelines for parents in working with their children:

1. Free yourself of the mistaken notion that you should "control" the child's behavior.
2. Accept responsibility for changing your behavior first rather than the child's.
3. Respect children for making the choices they can under the circumstances as they perceive them.
4. Realize that children are attempting to make a place for themselves by whatever means seem available to them (a useful or useless behavior).
5. Understand that when children misbehave, it is an outward sign of their internal discouragement as participating members of your family.
6. Commit yourself to helping children learn self-discipline and cooperation by friendly participation in the daily tasks everyone must fulfill.

The Goals of Disruptive Behavior

Children misbehave for a reason. Virtually all disruptive behavior can be divided into four goals, whether children are conscious of them or not:

1. Attention-Seeking.

While everyone seeks attention, this child demands it constantly. He or she believes, "I only count when I am being noticed or served." The attention-seeking child's behavior can be either active or passive. Active attention-seeking includes bothering others, showing off, performing mischief, constantly asking questions (often meaningless), and "clowning around." The passive child is often shy, nervous, lacks confidence, may have a speech problem, is messy, worries, and manipulates others to do things so that he or she will not have to do them.

Most parents slip into the traps laid by these children. They punish, nag, coax, remind, advise and give service. When the child receives enough attention, he or she will be satisfied. But the satisfaction is always short-lived and the child soon resumes the negative behavior.

We recommend that parents, instead of nagging or arguing, ignore the child or do the unexpected. Above all, parents should not show their annoyance, but be firm with the child and give attention and praise for correct behavior rather than responding to the negative actions.

2. Power-Seeking.

Children discover early that they can say "no." Some can be stubborn and challenge adults. The power-seeking child believes, "I only count when I am dominating, when I do what I want to do."

Typical actions of the power-seeking child include arguing, contradicting, continued rule breaking, temper tantrums, dishonesty, and general goofing off." Passive acts include being lazy, stubborn, and forgetful.

Parents who slip into conflict with the power-seeking child must approach the problem with calmness and persistence. Merely denying the child what he or she wants, however, usually leads to intensifying the conflict. Parents must first admit that the child has the power to disrupt the family. After this, the parent must be firm and maintain order. He or she should avoid engaging in a power struggle, arguing, or showing anger. Rather, he or she should be consistent in action and attempt to stimulate proper behavior.

Bedtime is a prime battleground. Many parents of power-seeking children find themselves begging their children to go to bed. The angrier the parent becomes, the more stubborn the child becomes. Soon tears are flowing, and many parents give in. As soon as they do, the child wins.

To avoid this, parents should firmly state the hour for bedtime earlier in the evening. There are no exceptions. The child is put to bed at the assigned hour and kissed good night. Whatever excuse the child gives is ignored. They may be hard to do at first, especially with the child crying, but after a few days or a week, the child will go to bed on time. Once he or she realizes that he or she cannot win, the game will be ended.

3. Revenge-Seeking.

The revengeful child is difficult to work with. His or her message to everyone is, "I can't be liked. I count if I can hurt others as much as I hurt."

Typical actions of this child include cruelty, stealing, bed-wetting, fighting, and being a sore loser. Passive behavior includes moodiness, rebelliousness, threats, and withdrawal.

Parents of this type of child usually feel deeply hurt, which is exactly what the child wants. If the parents punish the child, he or she will seek retaliation or may rebel entirely. Parents must retain order with minimal restraint, and show this child that he or she is liked, and that the parents want to spend time with the child.

4. Inadequacy.

This child says, "I can't do anything right and I'm no good. So I won't do anything at all."

Most actions of these children are passive. They give up easily, rarely participate, and project a helpless image.

Most parents of these children are at a loss how to help them. "I don't know what to do" is a common response. The child who feels inadequate needs support and encouragement. Parents should eliminate all criticism and offer every possible encouragement, no matter how small. Parents should not show pity to this child, but rather focus on his or her strengths as a way to build confidence.

Along with understanding the basic motives and actions of children, parents should also try to understand the reactions of children to remarriage and a stepfamily. The loss of one family and the blending of the family cultures with those of a new one can be hard for children.

Young and Pre-School Children

Young and preschool children are perhaps the most adaptable to changing family conditions. When parents are concerned and willing to work for their children's welfare, these children can make relatively easy adjustments both to the divorce and remarriage of parents. However, when there is much animosity between the ex-spouses, the children may become confused and depressed. They do not have the experience to cope with the unsettling bitterness of the parents' anger.

Still, when a child is very young, a caring new parent can fill the void of the absence of the biological parent and a close relationship can be established. Parents must realize, though, that the concepts of divorce and remarriage will be difficult for the child to understand, and he or she may mourn the loss of the real parent far longer than an adult would. Parents should observe the child's behavior closely, because it is not unusual for young children to seek attention by retreating to babylike behavior.

If contact with the non-custodial parent is not positive, the child may become resentful, feel guilty that he or she is somehow responsible for the divorce, or blame himself or herself for driving his parent away. Children in such situations need even greater support and encouragement from the stepfamily so that they can make a positive adjustment. If necessary, contact with the non-custodial parent should be limited. The child's emotional well-being should be a primary consideration during visitation.

The most important act parents can do for young children is to listen to them, answer questions sincerely, and show consistent love. This love should come from all the parents. If the child feels accepted and a part of the new family, separations, new brothers and sisters, and new households and lifestyles are much easier to manage. A child of this age seeks caring and stability, something the stepfamily needs to, and can, provide.

Elementary School-Age Children

Children of elementary school age may find the adjustment to the stepfamily harder than younger children. The emotions of elementary school-age children are easily seen and shown and can cause parents much heartache. Because boys and girls are already quite attuned to sex roles, their reactions to the process of divorce and the establishment of a stepfamily can be vastly different.

Girls at this age are usually close to their mothers and strongly model many of their mother's behaviors. They are maturing and identifying their sexuality and may even compete for the attention of a new father. Sometimes they will be vocal (usually more than boys) and express what is on their minds—if not always with clarity, with much emotion.

Some girls of this age may grow up too fast, and assume roles beyond their capabilities. This happens often when they are living with single fathers. In this regard the child may become a type of girlfriend and act more the role of an adult than a child. This can lead to trouble, especially when the father starts dating and the daughter views her father's girlfriends as rivals. Keeping the role expectations of a child at a normal level of development is important, not only for the child but also for the welfare of the family.

As girls tend to identify with their mothers at this age, boys identify more with their fathers and are usually proud of their accomplishments. While they may be less vocal than girls, boys may also be angry or confused about the divorce and subsequent remarriage and stepfamily. Although there will be times these children will act grown-up, parents must remember that they are still children and need their support and love.

Children of this age expect the world to be "fair and just" and will want the house to be run accordingly. Of course, like most children, their ideas of what is fair and just may differ from that of their parents. These children need structure and will test whatever rules their parents put forth. If the parents experienced problems with their children before a remarriage, those problems will probably worsen afterward. Not only must the old problems be solved, but the new ones brought on by the remarriage must be addressed and managed.

A vital step parents can take to help elementary school-age children adjust to the stepfamily is to make sure the children know what is expected and allow for emotional discussions. As with preschool children, elementary school-age children may also be slow in grieving for the loss of their natural parent.

Even though the adults have moved on to new relationships, the children may still be confused, particularly if the non-custodial parent is seen infrequently, or is unable to maintain a positive relationship with them. Sometimes, the children grow defensive and come to idolize the missing parent, overlooking any faults and magnifying the parent's goodness. They may also show anger at the stepparent because he or she has taken the place of the biological parent.

Teenagers

Teenagers can be hard to live with even when a family is undergoing no crisis. Teenagers like things "their way" and usually do not want their lives disturbed. They are "I" centered and interested primarily in themselves. Divorce, remarriage and becoming a member of a stepfamily is a troublesome adjustment for many teenagers.

A problem we frequently encounter is parents giving their teenagers full adult status in the family. They allow the teenage child to make major decisions. This is almost always a mistake; remembering how you were as a teenager will give you a perspective of this situation.

Many teenagers are permitted to choose the parent with whom they will live after the divorce. While input on this question is good, the ability of a teenager to make this very difficult decision should be analyzed. Does a teenager have the experience and the ability to stand back from emotion to make the right choice? Who can best determine the welfare of a child? The parent or the child?

Since teenagers are caught in the middle of a developmental struggle (Am I adult or child?), they may bicker and argue with family members in an effort to assert their independence and freedom. They will undoubtedly commit some obvious mistakes and may lack a mature sense of judgment, though they will bitterly deny any immaturity.

Chapter 14 — Understanding Children's Behavior

Teenagers in a stepfamily can be like a whirlwind. Feelings and words can get out of control as the teenager's life gets more and more frustrating. They will demand more freedom, but that freedom seldom brings joy or stability. Indeed, it will often lead to more chaos because the teenager is not mature enough to manage the independence he or she craves.

Without question, adolescence is also a difficult time for the parents in a stepfamily. Teenagers consistently push the rules of a family in order to understand themselves and to assess the parents' commitment to the relationship. There is never an easy answer or way to determine if the teenager is ready for more independence. We always tell the parents of teenagers: "Trust your instincts. If you think the child is not ready for a specific experience, then you are probably right. Let your children earn their independence."

When conflict arises because of the teenager's behavior, the parent must intervene and explain why the behavior was inappropriate. Dr. Howard Hensen of St. John's Hospital in Santa Monica offers some sound suggestions:

1. Do not raise your voice when you are angry at your child. Your displeasure can be communicated without unduly frightening your child.
2. Never swear at a child or call a child names.
3. Avoid using unnecessarily harsh language.
4. Think before you speak. You cannot take back cruel words. Once you have said them, the damage is done.
5. When you are very angry, take time to cool down before talking to the child. Leave the room and count to ten or take time to evaluate how the situation should be handled.
6. When disciplining your child, talk about the specific behavior. Example: "I don't like it when you..." This allows the child to understand exactly what he did wrong so that he will not do it again.
7. When you are upset at your child's behavior, explain the reason for your concern. Your child may not act rationally, but as an adult you can explain why he or she must not continue this behavior.
8. Remember to praise a child frequently. If you do not tell your child how great he or she is, who will?

9. Tell your children you love them. They need to be reminded, especially when you are unhappy with them. They need to know that you can be unhappy with them but you will always love them, no matter what.
10. Always provide privacy for discussions. Just as any adult would find a public dressing-down humiliating and distressing, so will your child. He or she will listen better and understand what you are saying more if you are alone.

While determining a proper balance between freedom and structure is important, the integration of children from two sets of families may be a paramount concern. Teenagers of the opposite sex may be sexually attracted to the new spouse, or even to each other. It is generally a good idea to discuss such issues openly so that everyone involved knows what is occurring. Understanding the emotions and feelings will make it easier to deal with them.

Teenagers are in a developmental crisis in any family, and becoming a member in a stepfamily only heightens this struggle. Helping teenagers understand what is happening to them, as well as the changes that are occurring because of the stepfamily, will help them to find themselves and also secure their place in the stepfamily.

Chapter 14 Understanding Children's Behavior

Adult Children

While one may expect the adult child to be more understanding of his or her parents' divorce and remarriage, this may not always be the case. Rejection of a new spouse or stepfamily by adult children is not uncommon.

> Amy, a woman in her forties, relates her story, which is quite typical. "When I left John, I felt very confused and guilty. I sought help and acceptance from my parents and children, and everyone seemed to be obliging. My son was stationed in Europe and he felt that if I thought what I was doing was okay, then he would support me. My mother also agreed. The problem came when I called my son in Houston. He got very angry and literally began yelling at me. It was very confusing to me and I got angry myself. "Of all my children, I thought he would understand more than his brother. I guess I was wrong. Finally I told him that I was going to do what I wanted anyway, even if he didn't like it. I'm not going to let him bring me down. So, we haven't talked in a long time and now that I'm remarried, he is even more resentful."

Certainly not every case is like Amy's, but many resemble hers all too much. Just because one's children are adults does not mean that they will understand or approve of what has happened to their parents' marriage. When their parents remarry, the hurt can deepen.

Parents should make every attempt to explain to their adult children why they are divorcing or remarrying. Sometimes a frank discussion is all that is necessary. Sometimes, it may take months, or even years for adult children to accept the change in their parents' lives.

When informing adult children of the plans to divorce or remarry, parents should keep the following points in mind:

1. Bring the subject up when the parents are ready. If the parents are not ready, or if they feel uncomfortable or are not sure what to say, they should not say anything. Starting something that one may not be prepared to finish is a mistake.

2. Parents should be honest but reveal only what they think is necessary and worthy to discuss. Nonessential facts will only cloud the issue.

3. Parents should be understanding. The children are likely to be upset. After all, the parents are disturbing their world regarding holidays, phone calls, the parents' availability, and their feelings that their parents are steady and unchanging.
4. Parents should expect children to feel sorry for what has happened and let them grieve.
5. Parents should expect resistance to a new spouse or children.
6. Parents should assure their children that they love them.

With adult children, parents must be truthful, and also must be willing to accept the objections of their children. They may be adults, but that does not mean that they will be able to set aside emotion and view the changing condition of their family without anger and confusion. Parents of adult children, however, should not permit the attitudes or feelings of the children to influence their decisions. The parents have a responsibility to take charge of their own lives and must do what is best for themselves. The children should never be permitted to dictate terms according to which the parents should live.

Most stepfamilies have children. In most, the children come with the mother. In some, they come with the father. In others, they come with both new parents. Many husbands and wives in stepfamilies may have children of their own, giving these families an interesting assortment of stepbrothers and stepsisters.

The stepfamily, by its very nature, places pressure on children, compounding and exaggerating the ordinary issues of growing up. The parents in stepfamilies need to make a strong and consistent effort to understand their children and help them to cope with the confused feelings and powerful emotions they are likely to experience. When parents understand the behavior of their children, and help their children to become better adjusted, contributing members to the stepfamily, all family members will benefit.

Chapter 15
The Effects of Relatives, Professionals and Society on the Stepfamily

A major problem for the members of stepfamilies is the demands others make on them. These demands often begin before the remarriage.

During the divorce proceedings, relationships among both the nuclear and extended family become strained. The husband's relatives rush to his side; the wife's relatives support her. By the time the legal battles have ended, little consideration for the ex-spouse's side of the family is left. Sometimes, the relatives can cause as much, if not more, pain than the ex-spouse.

Lawyers usually strain the relationships further. We have seen this happen even when spouses thought they were friends and hoped to go through with their divorce amicably. As the lawyers grapple over the division of property, relatives invariably become involved and offer advice that only confuses the process.

Children, too, are drawn in, often becoming pawns used to hurt the ex. Many spouses will say that they will do "anything for the kids," but too often decisions are made in the self-interest of the adult. In such cases, everyone suffers.

Joint custody, for example, has been praised as the only viable option for divorcing parents with children. It is touted as a way that even parents who constantly bicker will learn to solve their problems. Unfortunately, joint custody for some parents is a serious mistake. Instead of encouraging the parents to work together for the benefit of the children, the parents fight just as much as they did when they were married. Even therapists who are living with joint custody arrangements have trouble making it work.

In our practice, we see many of the same problems with joint custody. Following are the four most common:

1. The children are shuttled back and forth between houses like suitcases. This may work when the children are young, but usually does not once they reach school age. Children come to resent not being able to stay in one place where they can be with their friends. Children who are shuttled frequently between mother and father spend the greater part of their time with their parents, and often have trouble making friends with children their own age.

2. When the children visit the non-custodial parent, he or she often finds that much of his or her time is spent entertaining them. Many parents resent this. The time the children are with them is chaotic, while the time the children are away can be empty and lonely. Moreover, once children become involved with school, they usually prefer stability and dislike moving around. They may come to resent visiting the parent.

3. Ex-spouses need to be able to talk and communicate with each other at a friendly level, but because of joint custody they are constantly arranging shared schedules and appointments. While this is not only difficult and painful for many people, it can become even more troublesome when one person remarries. Remarried families and joint custody are indeed a difficult combination for those who do not have close relationships with their ex-spouses. It is often hard enough to plan and figure things out without having to involve a new spouse. Sometimes therapists can help prevent these situations from getting entirely out of hand.

4. Parents must live near each other during the years that the children are growing up. Since the average American family moves every three years, this can be a problem. When the parents are career-oriented, it is probable they will have to

pass up important career opportunities to continue the joint custody arrangement. However, this can result in resentment and the children may end up staying with babysitters as the parents juggle their schedule of parenting and job.

Contrary to the opinions of many therapists, we feel that joint custody requires great commitment and skills in communication. It is a decision that demands considerable foresight and planning. When joint custody works, it can be a productive parenting arrangement in which parents and children benefit. However, when it fails, everyone is hurt.

Remarriage and the Relatives

Remarriage often strains the relationships with relatives. The problems associated with making the new spouse a welcomed part of the extended family, taking care of the children in two families, dealing with old and new grandparents, uncles and aunts can become quite a chore. Besides understanding these folks, the members of the stepfamily must also listen to their opinions and advice. It is not surprising that the members of many stepfamilies feel like they are being pushed and torn in a hundred directions.

While most extended family members try to be open-minded and helpful, some can split the new family apart.

Jackie, a new mother of three, felt caught in the middle, being tugged from every side.

"It seems like everyone always wanted to tell us what to do," she explained. "It's hard enough with two sets of grandparents but we had four sets that were very vocal. Each one was bossy and demanded to have the children for vacations and holidays. It got to be so ridiculous that Phil and I argued all the time. It wasn't until I left for a while that we started to set our own priorities."

In addition to family members, people tend to form new relationships or break old ones with friends from the past. After a divorce, one may lose contact with many friends who were an important part of the life with the ex-spouse. For many people, the reason for this seems to be that single individuals have trouble keeping relationships with couples. Where once it was two couples, now it is a couple and a single. It is not the same. Many singles feel uncomfortable going out as a threesome. As the single person starts to develop new friends, many of whom are in the same circumstances, he or she will drift farther away from former friends.

When the single person remarries, it becomes hard to keep his or her single friends. Now this person gains new friends once again, usually couples. He or she has a long list of lost married friends and lost single friends. As a remarried couple, the husband and wife usually look for friends who have experienced what they have. Many adults of stepfamilies have friends who have been through divorce and remarriage, because they can understand these people, who in turn can understand them. Most therapists know that the majority of help in our country comes from the informal network people establish with friends and relatives. They help put the world into perspective. We have found that couples who have the most trouble in their marriages lack these informal networks. They are all alone and lose the perspective of reality in which caring for someone is essential.

While it is important for couples to be friends with other couples who have similar experiences, we also feel that they need to cultivate individual friendships. Partners should establish friendships at work, through private and community organizations, and church. Rather than detracting from a relationship, individual friendships can enhance a person and add interest to a marriage. A balance of mutual and individual friends can provide important emotional support to a couple.

Society and culture can also have a major impact on the stepfamily. Stepfamilies constantly receive messages—some subtle and some quite pointed. One is that stepfamilies, because they are not traditional, are second-best. Another is that the children of stepfamilies will not be as successful as the children of traditional families. While neither statement has been proven, they cause much insecurity for many adults in stepfamilies.

Let us examine the statement of the children of stepfamilies not being successful. There are so many influences upon a child today that it is difficult to say which has the most impact. We do know that good, caring families are helpful to both children and adults. We think it is easier for children when both parents are present in the home as models. However, non-traditional families can be very successful. We know of many cases in which a single parent is doing a fine job of raising his or her children. Stepfamilies, too, when anchored by caring parents, can provide

Chapter 15   The Effects of Relatives, Professionals, Society

a positive environment for children and help them to become responsible adults. In this regard, stepfamilies are like any other family. In the final analysis, the best way to develop a healthy stepfamily is to have parents that are caring, have a strong marital bond, and extend their love to each and every child whether step or biological.

Society's Impact on the Stepfamily

The members of stepfamilies must not only cope with the pressures that result from the blending of families and personalities, they must also withstand the influence and demands of society. Certain groups can exert a powerful impact on stepfamily members. Indeed, these people, if their negative demands, advice, and suggestions are taken to heart, can destroy the stepfamily. We will examine the most important of these groups one by one.

1. Lawyers.

It seems that whatever one does or changes in a stepfamily, a lawyer must be consulted. While this is of course a generalization, it is not far from the truth. Most folks in stepfamilies come to feel as though they are supporting lawyers for life. Many also believe everything that lawyers tell them, and fear to make decisions without the advice and approval of their legal advisors.

While the advice and help of lawyers is important, members of the stepfamily must also realize that there are many decisions that they themselves must make. In addition, there are many practical reasons why people should deal with their lawyers carefully and weigh the legal advice they receive scrupulously. The more one calls his or her lawyer, for instance, the more expensive the lawyer's bill. Further, lawyers work on an adversarial system—they play to win—but this can be detrimental to relationships. Although the client may be only looking for a simple solution, his or her lawyer is out to win all that is possible. It is not uncommon for a lawyer to win the battle while his or her client loses the war. On top of all this, most lawyers seldom do preventative work and generally deal with problems after they occur when they are harder to solve. Finally, some lawyers, the less principled to be sure, actively practice law in a manner that insures that their clients keep using their services. Thus, as long as the client's problems are never fully solved, the lawyer is assured of continued business.

We have seen many stepfamilies aggravate their problems by taking questionable advice from their attorneys. The result, unfortunately, is a continuation of the problem rather than a solution. Following are some typical examples in which we have heard lawyers prove to be more of a hindrance than a help to the people they represent:

- The lawyer demands outrageous child support payments or seeks more money constantly from an ex-spouse.
- The lawyer allows the ex-spouse too much freedom in seeing a child, or too little time.
- The lawyer negotiates endlessly over minor, or senseless, issues for years.
- The lawyer lets an ex-spouse run roughshod over his or her former partner.
- The lawyer advises his or her client to remain in one place so as not to complicate the custody settlement.
- The lawyer refuses to obtain a second opinion on controversial matters.
- The lawyer never negotiates items that have changed such as income level needs of children, and so forth.
- The lawyer fails to act when a child's mental, physical, or emotional health is in danger.
- The lawyer minimizes the client's problems.
- The lawyer fails to provide the best alternatives for the client and the client's family because of personalities.

An example of how lawyers can complicate the problems of a stepfamily is the experience of Jack and Jill.

After the divorce, Jack is supposed to pay a small amount of child support for their son. He chooses to live nearby and, since visitation is not clearly stated, he visits as he pleases even when Jill has a date with her new boyfriend. Within a few months, child support becomes an obsolete item because Jack claims that he can no longer afford it. However, he continues to see his son as much as he wishes. Jill contacts her lawyer about this, but, burdened with several other cases, he is reluctant to take on another and suggests that Jill threaten Jack with court. However, this is an empty threat. Jill does not want to pursue the matter because of the financial and emotional expense it would entail. The situation lingers on.

Chapter 15   The Effects of Relatives, Professionals, Society

> *After two years, Jill remarries. Joe, her new husband, becomes actively involved as a father. He wishes to adopt Jill's son because of his love and his steady financial support. Jill approaches Jack with this idea, and he defiantly says, "No way!" Jill then seeks a lawyer to determine her rights because of nonpayment of child support money. Jack, naturally, proceeds to get a lawyer and the fight begins once again.*
>
> *Had Jill's lawyer acted swiftly and decisively when she first went to him for help about the nonpayment of child support, it is likely she would not have had to go to him regarding the adoption. Confronted by a fair and forceful attorney from the start, Jack's behavior would have been held more accountable and he probably would be more open to compromise.*

With nearly 25 percent of non-custodial parents refusing to pay child support, these circumstances are often more real than imaginary.

When the members of a stepfamily go to a lawyer for help, they must understand what their lawyer is supposed to do, what he or she can do, as well as what he or she cannot do. If they are now sure how a lawyer can help them, they should ask. Knowing how much their lawyer can do for them enables people to use their lawyer to their advantage.

Without question, lawyers provide a valuable function in our society. Our only caution is that the members of stepfamilies use this service for their benefit. People can make decisions without the help of a lawyer if they work to keep their past and present relationships on friendly terms. Acting as mature and caring adults models important behavior for children. Arguing, ranting and screaming for revenge, and making threats leads to disaster for the children and their parents.

> *Lawyers must understand what is in the best interests of their clients, and it is the responsibility of their clients to tell them what those interests are. When the members of stepfamilies feel that their lawyer is not on their side, they should hire another one. There are plenty of lawyers around for all of us.*

2. The School System.

Most schools are cooperative when working with stepfamilies to solve problems. Previously, we discussed using the family name for the child's last name, even if that name is not the legal one. This often makes it easier on children, and many schools are willing to comply with the custodial parent's wishes on this issue. All problems are not so easily resolved, however.

Schools sometimes wind up in the middle of disputes between ex-spouses. For example, the non-custodial parent may decide to observe a child in school without informing anyone. Or he or she may simply show up one day to take the child home. Either case will likely make the custodial parent and school officials uneasy, especially if there is a problem regarding custody or visitation rights.

Teacher-parent meetings are another area in which teachers can find themselves in the middle. We have seen sets of ex-spouses and stepfamily parents arguing about "their" child's education while the teacher is forced into the hapless role of referee. Issues like this should be resolved before they occur. Bringing family problems into the school and using the schoolroom as a battleground can be hopeless for all involved.

> Meg, a new mother of two, agrees. "I used to blame everyone for our problems: my ex-husband, the teacher, the school, and so forth. It wasn't until I realized that I had to get things together in our family that Judy started to change. She was just acting out because her father and I were having problems and I was too blind to see. She was receiving the hurt that should have been between her father and me."

Sometimes schools find themselves in the middle because they put themselves there. Some school administrators and teachers do not like the inconvenience of dealing with all the "parents" of children of stepfamilies, and they refuse to send each parent materials and important information regarding the child. In the classroom, treating the child as someone who is damaged or different does not help the self-concept of the child and may be detrimental. This is what is frequently wrong with special groups or programs for children of divorced parents. The children are treated as if they are not as good or competent as the other children. While we agree that it is important to help children with problems and provide opportunities to share difficulties so that solutions can be found, it is not always a good idea to stigmatize children by setting up special groups.

Parents must take the initiative in dealing with the school. When they are having problems with their children at home, they should notify the school. Possibly teachers or school counsel-

Chapter 15   The Effects of Relatives, Professionals, Society

ors are seeing the same behavior in school and may be of help in resolving the problem. If the child's teacher or counselor calls and explains that he or she is having a problem, the parent should be willing to work with this person in modifying the child's behavior.

Parents should also try to have their children put in classes with teachers who respect stepfamilies and their special needs. A teacher who is biased against stepfamilies, or who contends that they are no different than other families, may not be able to provide the type of program that the child of a stepfamily will excel in. At the worst, such a teacher can aggravate problems with which the child or family may be grappling.

In most cases, teachers are caring individuals who have a good intuitive sense about a child's needs as well as his or her family, and are willing to work with the child and parents. But even the best teacher needs help from the parents, and it is the responsibility of the parents to visit with their child's teacher and volunteer their help.

3. Grandparents and Relatives.

Although grandparents and relatives do not have visitation rights, in many stepfamilies they have a major impact. Here is the dilemma that many parents in stepfamilies must consider: Are the grandparents and relatives taking the stepfamily's development into account by their actions or are they merely seeking to gratify personal needs?

The parents of the ex-spouse, for example, may demand equal time with the children after the divorce. This often creates problems and keeps alive old family messages and traditions. In an attempt to be nice, the custodial parent can sometimes create a host of problems. Rather than insisting that the former spouse's parents see the children on the ex's time, the custodial parent may feel that he or she should share the stepfamily's time. This can be agreeable to the stepfamily if all members are comfortable with the decision, however, some stepfamilies prefer to spend more time with the new grandparents rather than the parents of the ex-spouse.

With custody and visitation, it is very hard for many families to get the time that they need and so they resent relatives taking the children away. Often grandparents do not realize that couples work hard and wish to spend summers and vacation time with their children rather than sending them to relatives. Also, the parents of the ex-spouse may not be supportive of the new family and may say things that are not supportive of the new husband and wife. When grandparents are negative in actions and words, they can cause great friction. The best solution is to let the ex-spouse share his or her time with the children rather than the time of the new family.

Grandparents and relatives may also put the stepfamily under strain by both overt and subtle nonacceptance of the new family, and especially the new spouse. Action and words may not fit together, and anger may eventually rise on both sides of the family. Following are some of the most common examples of nonacceptance:

- A spouse's parents saying they like the new spouse but then ignore him or her and condemn his or her actions.
- Grandparents or relatives relating (particularly during the holidays) how lonely the ex-spouse is.
- Relatives contriving to keep close relationships with an ex-spouse when it can be damaging to the new family.
- Grandparents refusing to understand how vacations are much different than before divorce.
- Relatives bringing up the past and reminiscing about old times at family gatherings.
- Relatives calling the mother of the children by her "old" name.

All of these, of course, are worsened when the husband and wife expect grandparents and relatives to immediately accept the new family, which in most cases is unrealistic. Relatives need time to adjust to the idea of a stepfamily.

To minimize conflict and tension with grandparents and relatives, it is important that spouses have "family discussions" with their own parents and relatives after the marriage. Many issues that would otherwise hang on for years and cause continued resentment and conflict can be resolved through open discussion.

It is helpful when grandparents or relatives accept the remarriage, but this is not always the case. If one's parents choose not to accept the stepfamily, they have that right. However, by not accepting the stepfamily, their child then has the right to change his or her relationship with them. Relatives who are detrimental

Chapter 15   The Effects of Relatives, Professionals, Society

to the stepfamily can cause much hurt because they are aware of the old family's "secrets." When they are not supportive of the stepfamily's decisions, we generally advise stepfamilies to limit and possibly curtail the relationship. We understand that this is a difficult act, but the survival of the stepfamily may require it.

> John discovered this dilemma through much pain. "I always wanted my parents to accept Lenore but it never seemed to happen. They never did forgive me for getting divorced because they just loved my ex-wife.
>
> "Well, they would ignore Lenore when we had conversations and would tell the kids to do the opposite of whatever she said. At first, Lenore and I argued constantly because I kept sticking up for my parents. Eventually, I saw what was happening and confronted my parents. Of course they said it wasn't true but their denial seemed shallow to me. They were better for a while but things got back to being a hassle again. I just resolved myself to see them as little as possible and only do what I felt obligated to do. It's too bad it has to be this way, but when I'm pushed to making a choice, I will always choose Lenore. I'd be a fool to not do that."

Traditional holidays for families may also be a difficult problem. Usually, these are addressed in the divorce decree. If they are not explicit, we recommend that biological parents discuss how holidays will be spent and organized. We do not have any suggestions here other than ex-spouses should be fair and that the children should feel good about any arrangements. We advise families to celebrate two Christmases or two Thanksgivings if the children are to be absent for that specific day.

Thus, while the tie to the ex-spouse is maintained, memories for the new stepfamily can also be created.

We think it is important that stepfamilies set relationships on their terms rather than try to live up to the expectations of others. This does not mean that one abandons all of his or her relatives, but rather that he or she develops an "understanding" with the members of the extended family. This understanding is based upon specific criteria for a continuing relationship and includes:

- That relatives accept the family as it is.
- That the past is less important than the present.
- That the stepfamily has a right to develop its own family memories rather than relive and lament past memories.

- That the new spouse is accepted as one of the family.
- That the ex-spouse is not discussed unless the new spouses bring him or her up during a conversation.

Every relationship needs criteria to make it successful. Relatives can be a very supportive group if they are informed of the new couple's needs. In most cases, people hurt others because the ones being hurt do not speak up. Strong relationships are enhanced by communication, not by anger over unspoken words. We believe it is better to discuss painful issues rather than trying to avoid them.

Society

The stepfamily has trouble finding a niche in our culture. Even though one out of two marriages ends in divorce and millions of individuals are a part of stepfamilies, the place of the stepfamily is still uncertain.

This lack of identification tends to make the members of stepfamilies feel unwanted, out of place, angry, and sometimes depressed. They may even have trouble introducing their children, spouses, and their situation to others. For many, a stigma is attached to being a part of the stepfamily.

There is no easy solution to dealing with our society and culture. It is the task of the members of stepfamilies to be proud of their families, to tell people about their lives, both the positive and negative. Too often, people are complainers, and this leads to distorted perceptions on the parts of others. Members of stepfamilies need to stand up for their rights, and, if treated as an inferior persons, speak up. They have nothing to be ashamed of with others.

The members of stepfamilies can gain support and help from other stepfamilies. Talking with a person who is in the same situation can be most helpful. In therapy, we often use successful couples and families to help others. Sometimes the message is clearer when it comes from a peer rather than a professional. Stepfamilies experience many unique struggles, difficulties, frustrations, joys, and accomplishments. We encourage the members of stepfamilies to share their growth and experiences with others.

Chapter 16
Creating Your Own Future

In previous chapters we have shared many methods, techniques, and observations that can aid a stepfamily as family members strive to build unity and cohesion. We have focused on both strategies and values that can help family members survive the emotional upheavals that they inevitably will experience. The people involved in a stepfamily that is suffering turmoil often find it difficult to see beyond their current problem. However, it is important that the members of a stepfamily are aware that their present actions will affect the future. It is essential therefore to shape plans in the present with an eye on the future.

As it develops into a family unit, the typical stepfamily has many ups and downs. For most, this development is a slow process. Understanding the basic steps of the process can help people anticipate developmental needs and formulate their plans accordingly. For this reason we feel it is vital to outline the developmental steps that a stepfamily is likely to experience.

0 - 1 Month

This is both a time of havoc and excitement for the stepfamily. The married couple is still on the "high" of romance, while the children may be uncertain of what is going to occur. For many families, this is a period of disruption as family members are not sure how everyone fits in. This is also a time in which feelings are shared, some causing hurt and resentment that will lead to conflict. If the parents are uncertain and appear upset and confused, the whole family may suffer.

It is vital for family members to realize that the beginning of the stepfamily is a time for listening and sharing, as individuals try to find a place and build ties to new family members. People may not know what to call each other and limits must be set on what types of behavior are acceptable and which are not. Each person may seek a private space for retreat, a request that should be honored.

Family members should expect tears, anger, and discouragement, as well as moments of happiness during this first month. The husband and wife must provide a united front to the children. They should avoid arguing, bickering, or giving any hint that the new marriage will not last. Unresolved feelings toward ex-spouses are common, but these should be down played in the new marriage. There is no reason to relive the past; the new family has begun.

> Mary and George both felt the pain and excitement that accompanied their remarriage. Both experienced a painful divorce as they were the ones who were "left behind." Both had custody of their children with George having two teenage sons and Mary bringing her ten- and eleven-year-old daughters into the new family.
>
> Even during their courtship, few things were easy for Mary and George. Mary expected George to make up for all of her ex-husband's shortcomings, and George felt the same about Mary and his ex-wife. This was evident in two themes they kept expressing to each other. George would always remind Mary, "Never look at another man," while Mary would warn George, "Don't work overtime because you're a workaholic."

Sensing the uncertainty of their parents, the children quickly joined the battle. They fought with each other constantly in an attempt to determine who would dominate. They also tried to make Mary and George as unhappy as possible, and usually succeeded.

It was not long after their remarriage that Mary and George began to consider ending it. However, like most people who are desperate for a solution to an ongoing problem, they decided to try something different. They began to act as if nothing would ruin their marriage. They stopped fighting in front of the children and set down reasonable rules of conduct and courtesy that all family members had to observe. Even if the children were determined to make life miserable for them, George and Mary decided that they would not let them know they were successful. In time the new rules began to work and the family began to pull together rather than apart.

The beginning of the stepfamily is a time of change, yet it is also a time that sets the stage for even greater change. Taking control during the first month can make the changes that will follow easier.

2 - 4 Months

For most couples, life begins to settle down somewhat now, though the children may become more vocal and demand certain rights. Feelings of uneasiness about one's place, and the reluctance to show caring for other family members may continue. This is especially true in regard to the new parent who may be unsure of his or her role. Adding to the new parent's dilemma is the hesitation of the children to accept him or her. It is crucial now to work hard to make the family a strong unit. Sharing activities and helping people spend time together should be a priority.

As the family settles into a routine, the couple may feel that they have lost some of their freedoms and they must come to terms with vocational and home duties. If this adjustment becomes an area of conflict, other family members may use it as a means to gain their own goals. The children, for example, may still try to destroy the marriage if they believe it would be better for them. Presenting an image of security is essential even if the relationship is experiencing strain.

Len, an electrician, has tried to forget this crazy period. "Joy and I were so much in love that we forgot to talk about how the house would be run. I just assumed that she would be like my ex-wife, but boy was I about to receive a big surprise! Joy thought that we should share household duties and I had trouble understanding her point of view. I worked all hours of the day or night and I didn't feel like coming home and vacuuming. It wasn't too long before the kids got into the act. My teenage son said he didn't want to do it either, because I didn't help and he wouldn't do 'woman's work.' Before I knew it the whole house was in an uproar and nothing seemed to be going right. In the end I started to see her point of view, and we all started doing chores together. It's not the most enjoyable thing in life, but we seem a lot closer now."

The adults must lead the family during these early days and model appropriate caring and consideration for family members. They should teach by example. Encouragement, support, and compromise are the building blocks of success during this period of the stepfamily, which has been aptly described as being a time of chaos.

5 - 7 Months

This can be a fluctuating time for the stepfamily. If marital problems are occurring, they often reach a critical point now. The honeymoon is past and the realities of marriage may force the couple to re-evaluate their decision about marriage and think about its chances for working.

On the positive side, seeking closeness and establishing strong ties can also happen during this time. Many of the games that family members have been playing with each other are now understood, and it is up to each family member to work toward closeness. If family roles are still uncertain, they must be clearly defined.

There will be times during this period that the family seems to be doing fine, and suddenly a new problem appears. Many of these problems will be related to the children, who frequently are still not ready to fully accept the situation. Children may complain, but most parents find that the complaints are less frequent and demanding.

Still, this can be a hard time for the new parent. If he or she cares for the children, he or she will likely be working hard to become close to them. Unfortunately, the relationships seldom develop as quickly as the new parent would like.

> "I used to hate to hear the phone ring on Sunday mornings," Linda revealed. "Julie would get so excited talking to her mother, and I really resented it. I did all the work and she never talked to me like that. I talked about it to Glenn but he didn't understand how I felt. I guess it was something that I have been working out myself. I know that Julie cares for me, but it's tough to compete with an idol. She's made her mother bigger than life. I guess that makes it better for her to cope with it, but Glenn sometimes plays this game, too. If everything was so great, why did the two of them leave? When I bring it up to Glenn, he gets real defensive. Maybe I just want him to talk to Joy the same way about me as he does about her."

By the half-year mark, many stepfamilies have overcome the great initial adjustment, though problems still remain. They must continue to work hard for family growth.

8 - 12 Months

Most stepfamilies attain a sense of pattern and stability by this time. The children may be willing to show more affection, particularly if affection has been modeled by their parents. By now the new parent can be better understood and integrated into the family, which does much to reduce tension and conflict.

Although family rules may still be misunderstood, or ignored, by some members, and expectations between children and parents will differ, the foundation of the new family should be firmly in place. If it is not, it is probable that the family is experiencing serious adjustment problems. If therapy is needed, it will become obvious during this time.

We have found that many families come to therapy during this period because they have exhausted all possible solutions to their problems and have nothing else to try. Most of these families have missed many of the important first steps for beginning a healthy stepfamily, and the problems have piled up to where they are at a crisis level.

At this point, we work at helping the family reduce the crisis and start again. It is vital to initiate steps and establish rules that will enhance interaction and understanding in the family. For instance, if the children or a new parent are refusing to get involved with each other, we discuss openly with the whole family the reasons why this is occurring.

Family members must care for each other if the family is to evolve. Otherwise, a family identity will not emerge and the group will be little more than a collection of individuals who happen to live in the same house. Most members of stepfamilies desire closeness with other family members, but they do not know how to achieve it. Instead of helping each other, they may withdraw, fell misunderstood and hurt.

13 - 18 Months

It is during this period that many stepfamilies begin, finally, to make sense to their members. If ambivalent feelings are present on the parts of the children or a parent, this will of course hinder the family's growth, however, the healthy stepfamily is starting to function like a true family now. Adults with inadequate parenting skills because of a lack of experience will come to feel more comfortable, family members will understand and accept relationships, and the art of compromise and negotiations will have been learned.

If the family is comfortable as a unit, most problems that would have appeared as a crisis just six months ago now are easier to manage. Decisions that are made may not please everyone, but once tempers cool there is likely to be general acceptance. This is something that all successful families experience.

Thus, we see conflict as a part of every family. The problem is often how we deal with conflict rather than the conflict itself.

As families grow older, some developmental conflicts are inevitable. Many of these conflicts are a result of change. A newborn arrives, children become teenagers, a child leaves home, a grandparent dies—these are just some of the changes that happen to families.

The example of a new baby is a change that affects everyone in the family. Many times a couple in a stepfamily will have a child of their own. It may be an accident, or a planned event.

Sometimes, this is the reason the couple marries. No matter what the reason, a new child can have a dramatic impact on the stepfamily. For most it is either a strongly positive or decidedly negative event; there is seldom an in-between when a newborn arrives.

If a couple decides to have a child to keep their marriage or their family together, the child will probably cause the opposite. Whatever troubles the couple or family were having will be worsened by the baby.

> Mary, for instance, wanted to have a baby because Sam worked much of the time. When they were together it was usually an unhappy experience, and she thought that a baby would bring joy into their marriage. After the baby was born, Sam remained home more, but he and Mary continually argued and he was soon working long hours again. Because the baby needed more attention and more of Mary's time, she resented Sam being gone. Their fights became constant and bitter. Even the baby received the brunt of their anger if he cried or misbehaved. Finally, Mary and Sam left their marriage, angry at each other and the baby. When a couple is not ready for a child, a baby can break a marriage.

However, a baby can also bring a family together. The baby can be a strong binding force between husband and wife, and can certainly be a joyous and beautiful experience. If a couple is willing to work together and share the responsibilities of a child, a baby can be very good for a marriage. In a stepfamily, a new baby can also help bring the children together. Sometimes, it makes all family members feel more like a family. Everyone has something in common and much to share and talk about. If the family is ready, a baby can bring unity and happiness.

Every stepfamily must be prepared for change. When change is accepted as an inevitable part of life and is anticipated, people are usually able to manage it. When change is perceived as a threat, however, it can lead to conflict and crisis. Because the members of a stepfamily often feel unsure about themselves and their roles in the family, change, if not handled with common sense and sensitivity, can easily balloon into an event that threatens the marriage. If this happens, and the family is unable to resolve it, counseling is usually necessary.

Ralph and Judy are an example of a conflict that mushroomed into a crisis. Having been married five years, neither could agree on parenting. This conflict was glossed over until their son, Timmy, became a teenager. Ralph thought that he needed to be free to grow up like he, Ralph, did. Judy thought that Timmy needed less freedom and stricter rules, especially for his schoolwork where he was failing two subjects.

Being unable to agree on how to manage Timmy, Ralph and Judy fought over virtually everything the boy did. Timmy was caught in the middle and often was drawn into the arguments. Because his parents could not agree on what would be appropriate conduct for him, Timmy usually did whatever he wished. Eventually, he was arrested for drunk driving. This resulted in a bitter argument between Ralph and Judy. Losing his temper, Ralph hit Judy, who then left and sought family counseling in an attempt to solve the family's problem.

Even though healthy stepfamilies have become a unit by a year and half, problems still occur and must be managed. When problems are handled effectively, the solutions strengthen the family and result in even tighter bonds.

19-24 Months

It takes most stepfamilies about two years to achieve a state of normalcy. By this time, most painful losses have been assimilated, and, hopefully, life appears more positive. Most members of stepfamilies realize that they are different and are not re-created nuclear families. They have become aware of the pressures and situations that are unique to stepfamilies.

Honesty is a core ingredient of the family unit. By this time, the foundation has been laid where individuals understand each other and can give comfortable and positive caring. The pitfalls that can plague the family are visible and can be circumvented.

Although the stepfamily is running smoother now, it is not entirely without problems. Mary's teenage son, Ted, is a good example. Whenever he would not get what he wanted or would be disciplined, he would run off to his father's house. His attitude was: "I'll show you if you don't let me do what I want." Quite simply, Ted did not like any restrictions being put on him.

Mary and her ex-husband talked about the problem and worked out a solution where Ted would be allowed to visit almost any time, except when there was a disagreement at home. This continued for several years until Ted became 16. At that time, he requested to move in with his father. Since his father had not remarried, Ted received more attention and money when he was with his father than when he was with the stepfamily. It was painful for Mary, but she made the right choice for herself and her stepfamily and let Ted leave. For a time, he seemed to be happy. However, his father had to discipline him, too, and eventually his father remarried.

The Stepfamily in America

The nature of the stepfamily can lead to disorganization. Many people do not know how to manage the new roles and situations for which they have had no training or experience. Consider the child. Being a child is infinitely harder when one has two sets of parents, two homes, and various rules. The situation is ideal for resentment and anger.

Adults struggle with just as much confusion. They may resent not being close to "their' children and too close to others. Expecting to love someone immediately can be a major task for anyone. Trying to be a parent when no one treats him or her like a parent is no less tough. The new parent in the stepfamily is assuming roles that supposedly are reserved for biological partners. With the rate of divorce and remarriage rising in this country, people have no choice but to think, act, and feel differently about the stepfamily.

We believe that people can complain about their marriages and families as they fall apart, or take the initiative to make them work. There will be few people who greet the members of a stepfamily with: "Isn't it terrific that you have a stepfamily. I'm so proud of you!" More likely the comment will be something like: "Oh, a stepfamily. Is that like a real family?"

Divorce in America has only become a reality for most people during the last several decades. Although we agree that divorce is a devastating experience for most people, the process of ending and beginning relationships has changed dramatically. People are staying in relationships because it is a positive growth experience for them and not "for the children" or for everyone else.

Step by Step: A Guide to Stepfamily Living

National statistics reveal interesting trends. Less than 7 percent of all American families are traditional with the male as the breadwinner and the woman as the caretaker of the home and children. The divorce rate in America has quadrupled during the past 50 years, while the average family size has shrunk. Three out of four divorced women and five out of six divorced men eventually remarry, many within three years of their divorce. In 1989, the median age for second marriages dropped again to approximately 31 years of age for women and 35 for men. Many people are getting out of marriages while they are still young and hope that the second time will be more successful.

People in America are starting to believe that intimate relationships and family can be one of the most exciting aspects of life, or one of the most devastating. Too many individuals are unwilling to be psychologically, emotionally, or physically abused for the sake of society. The converse is also true. In a culture where everything is super-stimulating, people expect marriage to be like video games. People are looking for the perfect mate.

While most people have an idea about what a stepfamily entails, few of them understand the realities. They expect the stepfamily to be like a biological family, and then give up when they find it is not like that at all. Although there are similarities, the stepfamily presents people with roles that are quite different than the roles found in the traditional family. Still, there are similarities for any healthy family whether step or traditional. Here are some:

1. Partners share a marriage. They must be willing to work together.
2. Partners are (usually) parents. No matter what anyone says, they are parenting children in their home and possibly out of it as well.
3. Children can respect and learn to love their parents. Everyone, in fact, is lovable and can be loved. This may take time.
4. Parents have a life apart from their children. They should not dedicate their lives to their children, because children eventually grow up and leave.
5. Partners can build a caring and nurturing environment. This is what "family" means. It is a place where one is accepted for what he or she is.

6. Children have activities and lives that both parents can support and become involved in. Good parents take time out to be with their children alone as well as together.
7. Partners can have special memories and experiences. A stepfamily has more than its share of hardship, however, such experiences can make a family strong. Family members are reminded to learn to laugh at the "old days" rather than harbor past resentments.
8. Partners can become better spouses and parents as the stepfamily evolves and grows stronger. No one is perfect; everyone makes mistakes. Strength will come through experience.
9. As time passes, a successful family gets better. Family members must learn to compromise and live with each other. Time can be a healer of wounds.
10. Partners must keep a healthy mental outlook. They should not give up on themselves or each other and their ability to make life what they want it to be. The moment they stop believing in themselves, the family will also experience trouble. Success in anything demands hard work and perseverance.

Creating a family takes time. A family gives us security, caring and acceptance that the outside world cannot provide. A strong, loving couple will pass on positive values, behaviors, and attitudes to their children, not biologically, but rather through the sharing of time, experience, and life.

Stepfamilies can create happiness for the individuals involved. We believe any relationship in life that is worthwhile is worth the effort. Without effort, intimate relationships are difficult to nurture. To all those individuals living in stepfamilies and to the professionals who help them, we believe that stepfamilies deserve their fair chance; the opportunity to live productive lives surrounded by family members who love and encourage them.

Bibliography

Augsburger, D. (1980). *Caring enough to confront.* Scottsdale, PA: Herald Press.

Buscalia, L. (1988). *Living, loving and learning.* Los Angeles, CA: Slack Publishing Co.

Dreikurs, R. (1969). *Discipline without tears.* New York: Hawthorne Books.

Dyer, W. (1979). *Erroneous zones.* New York: Avon Books.

Dyer, W. (1983). *Pulling your own strings.* New York: Harper and Row, Inc.

Kalter, N. (1990). *Growing up with divorce.* New York: The Free Press.

Kern, R.M., Hawes, E.C., and Christensen, O.C. (1989). *Couples therapy: An Adlerian perspective.* Minneapolis, MN: Educational Media Corporation.

Rosemond, J. (1989). *Six-point plan for raising happy, healthy children.* Kansas City, MO: Andrews & McMeel.

Sweeney, T. (1984). *Adlerian counseling.* Accelerated Development.